Roman Mornings

ROMAN
MORNINGS

JAMES LEES-MILNE

*"The tourists tell you all about these things,
and I am afraid of stumbling on their language
when I enumerate what is so well known."*

P. B. SHELLEY

*"Cum subit illius tristissima noctis imago,
qua mihi supremum tempus in urbe fuit,
cum repeto noctem, qua tot mihi cara reliqui,
labitur ex oculis nunc quoque gutta meis."*

OVID

COLLINS
8 Grafton Street, London W1
1988

William Collins Sons and Co Ltd
London · Glasgow · Sydney · Auckland
Toronto · Johannesburg

First published 1956
This edition published in trade paperback
by Collins, 1988

Copyright in the revised edition
James Lees-Milne 1956 and 1988

BRITISH LIBRARY CATALOGUING IN PUBLICATION DATA

Lees-Milne, James
    Roman mornings.
    1. Architecture—Italy—Rome
    I. Title
    720'.945'632   NA1120

    ISBN 0-00-217936-9

Made and printed in Great Britain by
T.J. Press (Padstow) Ltd, Padstow, Cornwall

To
SACHEVERELL SITWELL
who looks at architecture
with the eye of a poet

CONTENTS

ILLUSTRATIONS

Introduction

WHEN at dusk the lanterns in the palace courtyards start glimmering and the church bells intoning those solemn, muffled notes that speak as though from the depths of the ocean, when the baroque folds of washing cease dripping over the narrow streets and the motor-tricycle drays, their parasols no longer sheltering mountains of violets and carnations but a stalk or two of either, snort their empty way homeward, when the smell of bleach and coffee gives place to that of fruit-rind and roasted chestnuts—that is the magical moment to wander about Rome. That is the moment to see the city of conflicting moods as it always has been and still is, hateful and holy, wicked and wise, pagan and papal, sometimes so beautiful that it is scarcely to be endured, and always quite inscrutable. That is the supreme moment to rhapsodize and pay homage, to make final assault upon the hidden secret of Rome's eternal decay, and to be deliciously deceived.

The early morning on the other hand is more to our purpose, for it is not at all romantic. All the conclusions of the previous evening disintegrate under the glare of Roman realism in a shower of useless fragments, like cheap glass roughly handled. It is the time to understand that you were seduced the previous evening by fantasies and to face facts. They present this piece of advice—that only until midday are you sure of seeing the insides of monuments; some may, others will not, be open again later in the afternoon; and this perplexity—that there are so many guide books all saying the same things in slightly different ways, some concisely, others at length, that it is a devilish problem to decide which to buy. The safe course is to choose the fullest and most concise, the one that combines the most information with the minimum amount of commentary. If there are two qualities to be eschewed in a guide book they are insufficiency and opinion. The guide book which describes a monument as "an edifice of the baroque period in the worst possible taste," or as "a mediaeval structure noted for the purity of its proportions" is to be avoided at all costs. What you need to be supplied with are simply bald data on which to build your own perfectly unbiased conclusions.

This small volume is in no sense a guide book; yet it is rather more factual than any guide book you will be able to buy. It can afford to be so because it only concerns itself with eight buildings in all. And since it is not a guide book it dares venture upon a few opinions.

Its purpose is quite straightforward. It deals with buildings representative of six phases in the architectural history of Rome. I am well aware that the phases I have chosen are somewhat random ones, and that there are others I have omitted altogether, like the Mannerist, of which Michelangelo was the shining exponent, and the Neo-classical, of which Valadier was a dim exponent. But the first phase did not put forth any immediate fruit in Rome after the death of Michelangelo, that solitary giant without a school, and the fruit of the second was not remarkable. None of my representative monuments is a ruin; for ruins are apt to display prettiness, picturesqueness and romance, qualities which evoke sentiments not concerned with a true judgment of architecture. Therefore I have deliberately chosen buildings in a fair state of preservation. Each of them, except possibly the representative of my last phase, is an architectural masterpiece which means something far beyond a mere building. That is the main distinction which interrelates them.

My monuments are accordingly creations of the best architects of their day. The names and personalities of the earlier architects are, unfortunately, either unknown or obscure. But there is one trait all these men from the ancient Roman myth Valerius of Ostia down to the rococo Salvi had in common, and that was a determination to remain traditional. They were steeped in the classical laws of architecture, to which they ostensibly adhered. And this is a primary reason why they were artists of power and originality. Their creations, as I shall try to show, are all archetypes, some, like the Pantheon and the Tempietto, more obviously so than the others. Indeed, individual features of these two temples are reflected upon buildings in practically every town of Europe, the Commonwealth and America. The influence of Rome upon the architecture of western civilization has always been more conspicuous than that of Athens.

The fact that my selection includes more religious than secular buildings is purely fortuitous. I do not prefer churches to palaces. But in Rome the first are more easily visited than the second. Besides only the first are representative of the three earliest phases which I have chosen to write about.

To judge architecture properly is scarcely less difficult than to create it. If you want corroboration of this statement consider the manifold standards of judgment which have been advanced, and discarded since the Renaissance. Consider some of the great scholars of the past, Serlio, Palladio, Fréart, Winckelmann, Ruskin, who have devoted lifetimes to determining whether good architecture is dependent upon the orders, mathematics, harmonics, anatomy or sexual propriety—and all in vain. Each succeeding generation has ridiculed the standard set up with so much earnest conviction by its predecessor. Today we are overrun with architectural historians. The good ones outnumber the good architects, to such a pass has the practice of this noble art declined. Owing to easy travel and photography contemporary historians have amassed wider factual knowledge than their predecessors ever boasted, so that there is a consequent tendency to judge architecture by standards too exclusively academic. The erudition of the least pretentious architectural student is quite astounding. He will rattle off the dates of birth and death of all our leading native architects without a pause; and he will ascribe an eighteenth-century portico or cornice to any season of any year, provided of course that the architects and buildings are British, for those of the Continent do not yet interest him much. This is a pity because in England classical architecture, unlike Gothic, is rarely first-rate, when we measure it by the abundance of excellence in Italy and France.

The somewhat narrow academic scholarship evinced by several of our contemporary historians need not, however, be wholly depreciated. It is after all one of the springboards whence many a deep plunge into architectural speculation is made. But in reaching a true assessment of architecture there are other values to be taken into account besides the purely documentary. Chief of them are the associative and the aesthetic.

Under the heading of associative value you must consider three several factors. They are history, environment and materials. Historic events may make profound impressions upon the spirit and character of buildings. Howsoever well preserved, buildings which are not inanimate or static things, change throughout the ages. After nearly two thousand years even the stolid Pantheon has altered. The wonder is that it has altered so little. "There are occasions," wrote Robert Byron, "when architecture resolves into history," and others when history resolves into architecture. No one will deny that different buildings express different qualities, so that in passing down a street you find yourself saying: This was the house of a great and good man, this of a family fraught with tragedy; before this church scenes of violence and carnage have been enacted; within this town hall grave men have deliberated matters of benefit to the human race. For instance, the buildings of the ancient Romans are seldom tender, which explains why certain critics have found them unpleasing and even repellent.[1] The Pantheon is extremely stern and sad. It has been the shrine of relentless deities, the refuge of warring pontiffs and, up to modern times, the scene of

[1] See A. Kingsley Porter, *Beyond Architecture* (Boston, Marshall Jones Company, 1928).

poignant incidents. When Raphael's corpse was laid in state within the rotunda the fat and cynical Leo X prostrated himself before it, and for the last time seized the right hand, which he bathed with his tears. During this remarkable display of homage the poor Fornarina, with whom the painter had lived faithfully for nine years, having previously been dismissed from the death chamber by cardinals and priests, was hounded from the bier by the self-righteous mourners. Events such as this have enhanced the melancholy ambience of the Pantheon. The Colosseum is essentially cruel. Within its arena Christians swathed in the warm and reeking skins of wild beasts have been torn to pieces by lions under the flare of human torches. The Piazza of Saint Peter's on the other hand is forgiving and welcoming. It stretches out its smiling arms to embrace the weary pilgrim who has walked barefoot from the far antipodes. The Villa Farnesina expresses sybaritic joys. It echoes with the splashing of gold plate into the Tiber, the pouring of wine into beakers and the laughter of wanton women. In other words violent emotional incidents and the slow repetition of events alter the character of buildings as surely as the Venetian cannon balls have left quick gashes on the columns of the Parthenon, or the wheels of Roman chariots over the centuries have worn indelible ruts upon the Via Sacra. It likewise follows, as Mr. De La Mare has observed, that buildings assume over the years some of the qualities of the people who have lived in and cared for them.

> . . . all things thou would'st praise
> Beauty took from those who loved them
> In other days.

The condition of a city's or a building's setting cannot be ignored in a comprehensive assessment of its architectural merits. You can no longer estimate the road to Rome through the eyes of Gibbon, as wearing silk knee-breeches and a lace cravat he rumbled across the Campagna in a travelling carriage, which was lined with Bedford cord and drawn by a pair of sweating horses. His preconceived notions of the Eternal City's aspect were governed to a large extent by the unbroken aqueducts, straddling across a landscape treeless and barren upon which brown, scorched sheep nibbled dry grass right up to the Porta del Popolo. Nothing else came between him and his furthest vision of the gnarled olive trees, like waves of amethyst washing the feet of Mount Soracte and the snow-capped Sabine Hills. These distant, indestructible images are still visible. But from the windows of your high-powered motor Mount Soracte has a different look with its great scar of a highroad slashed across it. The aqueducts are screened by electric pylons and long before you reach the Porta del Popolo the sheep have been replaced by flocks of glossy advertisements of Chlorodont and Vov, nibbling their way into Mussolini's cement suburbs. It is true that a glimpse of Saint Peter's dome may still be caught over the tops of the pylons and posters and the tenement blocks. But, whereas the first rapturous sight of it aroused in Gibbon—who was fundamentally a prosaic sort of person[2] —such "strong emotions" that he could "neither forget nor express" them, to you it appears—when it will appear at all through the mesh of suburban excrescences—a silver-grey gasometer that has lost its moorings and floated into the misty, powdery sky.

If then the spirit of a whole city can be altered, not incidentally by the loss of many monuments but by the conversion of its setting from a feathery wilderness of ineffable beauty to a rubbish dump under a network of wires, how much more drastic is the effect of transformed environment upon an individual building. We all know that one of the differences between a mere builder and an architect is that the first pays no heed to environment whereas the second makes it a part of his theme. The result is that we do not give a thought to the work of the first whereas we ponder over that of the second. A sense of the relationship of

---

[2] "My temper," wrote Gibbon in the famous Autobiography, "is not very susceptible to enthusiasm, and the enthusiasm which I do not feel I have ever scorned to affect."

architecture to environment was not exclusive to the renaissance architect. He first developed it into a positively conscious art and so gave us some highly interrelated examples like the Palace of Caserta with its terraces and cascades and the Château de Versailles with its long intersecting vistas and formal canals between pleached limes and trimmed hornbeam hedges. These buildings and their surroundings were purposely made so interdependent that it is impossible to conceive the reason for one without the other. Even the mediaeval architect was often dimly aware of the relationship when he placed his embattled castle upon a commanding crag and his half-timbered manor house within a moat. The proud castle deprived of its crag would in certain circumstances look pretentious and ridiculous: the defensive moat deprived of the chequered reflection of the manor house in its smooth waters would shrink to the status of an old dew pond in a field.

The relationship of architecture to landscape should never be ignored, whether you are contemplating a country house in a park, a palace in a street, or a church in a graveyard. It is, however, a factor which in the majority of cases makes the assessment of architecture today exceedingly difficult. For in nine cases out of ten where a building has not appreciably changed, its setting has altered out of all recognition. Always therefore in fairness to an architect you should before making a dogmatic pronouncement upon the merits of his work ask yourself what did the environment look like at the time when he was faced with the problem of building.

Architecture is the most vulnerable of the arts. Unlike poetry, music, painting (which, thanks to science, can now often revert to its pristine condition) and even sculpture (to which noses, fingers and other extremities can adroitly be restored) architecture cannot easily be patched, and yet look the same as before. Architecture does not keep still. It must always be changing, usually for the worse. It is maddeningly evasive. What then is the value of anybody's opinion of it, however perspicacious, since it is never the same from one year to the next? Whereas you are perfectly entitled to set Mr. Ernest Newman's opinion of a Monteverdi opera against Dr. Burney's, even to prefer Sir Kenneth Clark's opinion of "The Laughing Cavalier" to Hazlitt's, it will be a complete waste of time deciding whether Mr. John Summerson has a more just opinion of the merits of the Parthenon than Winckelmann had, simply because the Parthenon today is not what it was in the eighteenth century. Nevertheless do not suppose that Ictinus and Callicrates, the designers of the Parthenon, or the great architects of history who have followed in their footsteps, were unaware that the art they practised was subject to these distressing processes of change and decay. In a greater and less degree they most certainly were not. Accordingly they adopted the only means known to their experience of mitigating the effects of time, which was a careful choice of materials.

Of course they, as distinct from poets, composers, painters and even sculptors, must in the depths of their souls have questioned whether there was to be any permanence in their creations. But had they admitted as much to the world then they might just as well have practised some other art. For it is an acknowledged rule that a good architect must convey the impression that his work is eternal, whether it be of marble, stone, wood or lath and plaster. The Parthenon may look and be more solid than Little Moreton Hall in Cheshire, but the ricketty black beams and plaster fillings give this half-timbered house set in a hollow just as autochthonous an air as that conveyed by the Pentelic marble to the Greek temple on its Acropolis. Little Moreton Hall appears totally merged in its background, as though it has slowly sprouted, a monstrous vegetable growth if you like, out of the Cheshire orchards. And the reason why? Because the rude Tudor carpenters who pieced it together chose materials indigenous to their surroundings. An architect must adopt materials best suited to withstand the onslaughts of a particular climate upon his structure, and take advantage of the effects of sun and cloud upon his design. Pentelic marble under the leaden skies of Congleton and half timber under the blazing vault of Athens would not only weather exceedingly ill but look essentially incongruous, because they would not convey the desired impression of stability.[3] Little Moreton Hall, however soundly constructed on the Acropolis would forfeit all architectonic substance; so too would the Parthenon, reinforced by no matter what scientific subterfuge in a damp Cheshire water meadow. The only quality that either could possibly retain would be a pictorial one. And this quality in buildings is by itself not enough. A perfect, but sorry example of pictorial unreality is Matisse's new chapel at Vence, which is not architecture but a building that has stepped out of a picture (and not a classical but a post-impressionistic picture) and without the support of its frame looks about to topple down. It has no apparent substance and no form.

Form then is a quality to be more highly prized by architects than by the exponents of any other art. It is the prerequisite to every endeavour to produce a building of more than utilitarian pretentions. Form consists in the balanced and rhythmic relation of one elevation of a building to another, of the roof to the elevations, the windows to the doors and indeed of each separate unit to its fellow and to the whole. By its form the quintessential beauty of a work of architecture is estimated. It is the ultimate aesthetic value to which I referred at an earlier stage. Architecture is exclusively an abstract art. When poetry, music, painting and sculpture turn to the abstract they tend to become dull and vapid. The reason is that these arts are to a large extent representative or evocative of persons, things and sentiments. Entirely divorced from them they collapse into meaningless

---

[3] These words were written before I had seen the Minoan remains of Knossos and Phaestos where timber and plaster were apparently used. But a first-hand study of this horrible style has not made me revise my conviction that half-timbering is unsuited to the Mediterranean basin. To help conjure a picture of the Parthenon in Cheshire there is the begrimed, rain-sodden Penshaw Monument exiled on an industrialized moor near Sunderland.

scribbles, sounds, daubs or lumps. An architectural design on the other hand is only indicative of itself. It never expresses natural shapes; nor does it conjure up memories of objects or events. That it happens to be for a dwelling, church, factory or garage, is purely incidental to its importance as art. An architectural design does not represent a family, congregation, workmen or motor-cars, which a painting or piece of sculpture may do, nor evoke a noble aspiration or a nostalgic mood which an epic or a sonata may do. In other words the functional purpose which a building serves is not concerned with its aesthetic appeal.

The ancients and the men of the Renaissance in particular cared about form a great deal, the men of the gothic centuries less so. Their architecture was usually haphazard, not preconceived, but evolutionary. It had its own extraordinary virtues, so extraordinary that the world has not produced their like in any other realm of art of any other era—virtues which cannot be discussed here. We feel that gothic buildings are anonymous, are the products of innumerable ant-like minds and spider-like hands remotely controlled by some divine law. Although we know less about, say, Valerius of Ostia than about Henry Yevele—it is little enough—the Pantheon strikes us as less anonymous than the nave of Canterbury Cathedral. We feel that the first was the creation of one master mind, and the second the slow outcome of corporate effort. The architecture of the Renaissance was less anonymous still than that of antiquity. Italian architects in the fifteenth and sixteenth centuries emerged as positive individuals who usually proclaimed aloud what was in their minds and what were their aspirations. So their work means more to us than that of the old Romans. Because they gave us a measure by which to judge it we are better able to decide how far they were successful. That is why I have included the works of four of the greatest of these men in the following pages.

Since form is all-important it follows that architecture cannot be judged from illustrations. The most accurate photographs can only suggest the shadow of its real substance. Drawings and engravings can do better if the artists are capable of translating perspective and sculptural effects, achievements unknown to the camera. Architecture must be visited and looked at over and over again before an assessment of it can have any value. Furthermore it must be judged by the requirements and standards of its own time, to ascertain which is not always easy. It should never be condemned because it infringes those to which we may be accustomed. Because we live in a democratic state we have no right to call the Palazzo Massimo a piece of aristocratic frivolity. Because we are irreligious or puritanical we need not point a finger of scorn or disapproval at the lavish marble and gold of Sant' Andrea al Quirinale. We may be sure that our ideas of good government, and right and wrong were not shared by the great patrons of the Italian Renaissance or, for that matter, by the Roman Emperors. Yet they produced architectural masterpieces apparently far beyond our capabilities.[4] We are shocked, maybe, by their love of splendour and power. They would be appalled by our indifference to the architecture of our own time, to the meanness of our twentieth-century monuments and the hideous vulgarity of our streets. In these respects they would consider us very decadent. I think they would be quite right.

J. L-M. 1954

[4] We have yet to see whether the new Coventry Cathedral fulfils its promise to become the first concerted architectural masterpiece of our generation.

ANCIENT ROMAN

———◦◦◦———

The Pantheon

"AMONG all the ancient buildings to be seen in Rome, I am of opinion that the Pantheon (for one piece of work alone) is the fairest, wholest and best to be understood; and is so much the more wonderful than the rest, because it hath so many members, which are all so correspondent one to the other. . . ." These words were written by Sebastiano Serlio, the great legislator of architectural principles, in the third volume, issued in 1540, of his *Regole Generali de Architectura*. For two centuries and more the *Regole* was an indispensable text book for professional and amateur builders throughout the Continent and Great Britain, where it was first translated in 1611. Serlio went on to explain that the Pantheon was begun 5203 years after the creation of the world. Now I am perfectly ready to accept all Serlio's views, with only one exception, that the Pantheon is the "fairest" of the ancient Roman monuments. There can be no question that it is the "wholest" and least altered. On these accounts alone, apart from its remarkable construction, it is indeed "the most worthy of notice," to quote the words this time of an English admirer, John Evelyn, written in his diary just a hundred years later. That the world had been created precisely 5203 years previously I am not qualified to contradict. But "fair" is an adjective with which I do not feel inclined to endow this proud, stern, unsmiling memorial of Roman might and majesty.

The most striking approach to the Pantheon (on foot of course) is from the Piazza Capranica on the north-east, down the narrow one-way Via degli Orfani. At first you catch an oblique glimpse of part of a green, saucer-stepped dome, now of lead and originally covered with plates of gilded bronze, and of two columns of the portico which the early sun is bravely endeavouring to cheer. An impression of immensity is at once induced by this tantalizing, incomplete vision which as you continue walking gradually unfolds itself. But if you prefer your first view to be of the entire front elevation then there is only one approach which will allow it, and that is from the Via della Rosetta on the north-west. From slightly raised ground you may look down upon the Pantheon and see the vast pediment of the portico dominated by the equally vast pediment of the attic, the outlines of both serrated by sturdy tooth-like blocks (known technically as modillions), of which several missing ones have recently and quite rightly been replaced. For you must remember that until the Middle Ages the monument, now apparently sunk into the earth and much shrunk in size, stood on a raised platform of seven steps and enjoyed that necessary height which gave it the dignity it demanded. Moreover the space in front of it was originally far larger than the present *piazza*, and fittingly adorned with statues and busts of eminent Romans.

To make your way from one of the side streets into the Piazza della Rotonda is almost as hazardous an undertaking as paddling a canoe out of a placid tributary into the surging eddies of a whirlpool. At all times of the day and especially in the morning the *piazza* is turbulent with men, bartering, gesticulating and raising their loud voices in protest against the lusty clamour of the central fountain. In the nineteenth century the confusion was even greater for the *piazza* was the favourite resort of bird fanciers, vociferously proclaiming their merchandise. From hundreds of small wicker cages Java sparrows, native thrushes, robins, nightingales, linnets and ringdoves—all those species now practically extinguished by the Italian *cacciatori*—warbled their sad notes to the accompaniment of the cries of their captors. With skilful navigation you cut your way to the fountain, then climb the steps and take up a stance, leaning against the marble basin on the rim of which twin dolphins incline their heads lovingly against a satyr's mask. You inhale a delicious and peculiarly memorable aroma compounded of freshly ground coffee, cab-horse droppings and coppery fountain water. Before you the Pantheon grey and sombre broods imperturbable. There can be no better contrast to the gay and smiling architecture of the Greeks than this inscrutable monument. "I visited it several times," wrote Thomas Smollett, "and each time it looked more gloomy and sepulchral." "Simple, erect, severe, austere, sublime," Byron called it, "Shrine of all saints and temple of all gods"—and about the Roman deities there is nothing compliant or forgiving. This leads me to consider the purpose for which the place was built and the vicissitudes which make its survival so remarkable.

According to the inscription on the portico frieze the Pantheon was built by the famous statesman-general, Marcus Agrippa, during his third consulship in 27 B.C. But his Pantheon which was of rectangular plan was twice burnt, once during the reign of the Emperor Titus when it was little more than a hundred years old, and again—and this time disastrously—under the Emperor Trajan in A.D. 110. The second fire may have been caused by lightning,[1] or by the flames of the votive candles which the wind perhaps blew into the inflammable material draping the statues inside the temple. The statues before which hundreds of lights were kept burning represented the seven planetary gods and goddesses, the divine ancestors of Agrippa's intimate friend and father-in-law, the Emperor Augustus. For it was in his family's honour that the Pantheon had been erected after the naval victory of Actium over Cleopatra and Antony in which the Consul played a leading part.[2] The historian Suetonius tells us that many other splendid buildings, as well as aqueducts, sewers and granaries, were raised by the Consul at the Emperor's special request—"*a M vero Agrippa*

[1] Paulus Orosius—*Historiae*.
[2] Dion Cassius, however, says that Agrippa completed the Temple of Neptune to commemorate the naval victory of Actium, and that the Pantheon was erected in honour of Julius Caesar.

complura et egregia." However, the Emperor Hadrian was obliged completely to rebuild the body of the temple from the very foundations between the years A.D. 120 and 124. This fact was proved once and for all by the French architect, C. P. Chedanne when in 1892 he discovered that nearly all the bricks that compose the rotunda were stamped with a die of Hadrian's time.[3] How far the portico was altered to suit the new rotunda has not been satisfactorily established, but the inference is that the columns and entablature with the frieze on which Agrippa's words are deeply incised were reassembled by Hadrian.

For a comparatively brief period of its history Hadrian's monument served its regenerated purpose of a pantheon to the tutelary deities Jupiter, Mars, Venus[4] and their divine collaterals. A second inscription within the portico records that Septimius Severus and his son Caracalla were obliged extensively to repair the building—*"vetustate corruptum cum omni cultu restituerunt"*—about the year 202, which suggests a rather rapid neglect in the interval. By 399 we learn that the rotunda was once more in a bad way, closed as a pagan temple by imperial decree and abandoned. And so apparently it remained during the reigns of the later emperors absent in Constantinople. Then in 608 the saintly Pope Boniface IV procured the consent of the Emperor Phocas to consecrate the Pantheon a christian church in the name of Sancta Maria ad Martyres. The occasion was one of supreme importance in the annals of the Catholic Church. Hither the Pope brought from the catacombs twenty-eight cartloads of bones of early martyrs which he solemnly reinterred under the fabric of the new church. In the tribune, where previously

[3] Palladio believed that Agrippa added the portico to the rotunda, which belonged to the time of the Republic. Inigo Jones thought both portico and rotunda were built by Agrippa. Chedanne's researches have proved both partly wrong.

[4] The statue of Venus inside the Pantheon was like the other statues suitably dressed and covered with rare jewels. It wore in one ear half of the famous "union," an exceptionally large pearl, of which Cleopatra had dissolved and drunk the other half at a supper party to surpass the liberality of Antony. Among other statues, according to Palladio, was one of Minerva made in ivory by Pheidias.

incense had smouldered before a statue of Mars Ultor, Boniface raised a high altar to enshrine the Blessed Sacrament.[5] After the Feast of All Saints was fixed by a succeeding pope to take place on 1st November of every year, the Church, which has never hesitated to adapt profane traditions to Christian needs, rededicated the Pantheon of the pagan gods to the glory of its own elect. Hence we owe to the papacy the preservation of one of the most important buildings of the ancients although, alas, subsequent pontiffs cannot be spared grave censure for their systematic spoliation of the Pantheon in ensuing centuries. The next chapter in the history of the Pantheon is less edifying. In 663 the Byzantine Emperor Constans II who on a twelve day visit to his western capital plundered whatever he could remove of portable treasure, stripped the tiles of gilded bronze from the dome of the rotunda and put them on board his ships for Syracuse. Constans perpetrated this vandalism in spite of his protestations of reverence for the works of his ancestors and his membership of the Church under whose guardianship the building was now supposed to shelter. Over seventy years were to elapse before Pope Gregory III took pity on the ravaged monument by substituting a covering of lead. Nearly seven hundred years later we hear of Pope Martin V giving it yet another roof.

Before this last attention the Pantheon had throughout centuries of mediaeval turmoil lapsed into a fortress. In the eleventh century it was used by the anti-Pope Guibert as a stronghold whence he made periodic incursions against the lawful pontiff. In 1105 the anti-Pope Sylvester was elected within its defensive walls. In the fifteenth century the building was, as I have intimated, once more respected. Martin V's successor, Eugenius IV, tore down all the military fortifications and miserable dwellings which had accumulated like barnacles over and around the columns of the portico, and cleared out and paved a decent space before the monument.

---

[5] The present high altar was made by Clement IX (Rospigliosi), 1667–70, from marble taken from Domitian's Palace.

But the Renaissance was a period of lofty ideals not always followed by their originators. Noblemen of culture would present petitions to popes, who would issue bulls to the effect that historic monuments must be preserved on peril of dire consequences. Nevertheless the same nobles and the same pope would disregard their own injunctions by shamelessly despoiling what they professed to preserve. Thus the famous Barberini, Pope Urban VIII, who claimed to be the protector of the glories of Roman antiquity and was indeed one of the most enlightened and lavish art patrons to sit on Saint Peter's throne, completed the spoliation begun by Constans II. In 1632 he removed from the portico roof two hundred tons of bronze beams, ostensibly to lighten the weight of the decaying structure. Really it was in order that Bernini might recast them into the twisted columns of a handsome new baldaquin for Saint Peter's and manufacture from what was left eighty cannons for the papal armoury. One William Smith, a painter of burnished work from England, happened to witness the act. He was horribly shocked and when he got home told Inigo Jones who recorded his strong condemnation of the Pope's vandalism. Bernini added insult to this injury by building two little bell turrets upon the attic storey, which, although ridiculed by genera-tions of Romans as "orecchie d'asino," asses' ears, disfigured the façade until their removal in 1882.[6] Urban's indirect successor, Alexander VII, held the Pantheon in higher respect, albeit at the expense of other monuments. He replaced two of three decayed columns on the extreme left hand corner of the portico (the third, it is only fair to state, was a replacement of Urban's) by monoliths which he re-moved from the Baths of Severus Alexander, and restored parts of the pediment with marbles which he hacked from the mediaeval Arch of Piety than standing in front of the Pantheon. The motives of Pope Benedict XIV in the next

[6] Bernini's little bell turrets were probably suggested to him by those which Palladio put upon his rotunda church at Maser. Palladio's turrets were not afterthoughts, but integral parts of his composition.

century are less easy to appreciate, for he stripped the entire attic story inside the rotunda of its original pilasters and panels, and substituted a decorative scheme in every sense different and inferior. His action had the most drastic and disastrous effect upon the interior since it had been fashioned by Hadrian. The effect was not mitigated by the well-intentioned but distressing restorations of Pius IX in the middle of the last century.

Now what exactly is the Pantheon and what is its architectural importance? It is a round, domed structure, 142 ft in diameter and 140 ft in height, with a portico eight columns in width, stuck on to the front of it. Its marvel lies not, of course, in the portico, for porticoes were used in abundance upon Roman and certainly Greek buildings. It lies in the dome. But domes had previously been set upon Roman buildings, such as the Temple of Venus Genetrix[7] and the Baths at Baiae,[8] and even upon small Greek buildings before them, like the Choragic Monument of Lysicrates and the Tower of the Four Winds, both in Athens.[9] This is true, but never before in the recorded history of architecture had a dome existed of such colossal dimensions. The Pantheon dome has stood the test of over eighteen hundred years' assault from earthquake, tempest cannon and explosive. Hadrian's experiment in roofing was something entirely novel and amazingly bold. The great weight is carried on a mass of concrete, twenty feet thick, broken by eight large niches or openings. In other words the dome is supported not by an uninterrupted circular wall, but

[7] The Temple of Venus Genetrix, at Baiae, was octagonal and domed. It was 60 ft in diameter and its walls were 7½ ft thick.

[8] Il Truglio, Baiae, was circular. Its elliptical dome had a large circular eye over a drain. It was 66 ft 8 in. in diameter and was probably a *frigidarium*.

[9] The Monument of Lysicrates (335 B.C.) admittedly has a tiny cupola topped by a finial flower, and was formed of one entire block of marble. The Tower of the Four Winds (75 B.C.) is a larger structure than the last. Its roof covering is composed of twenty-four marble slabs slightly curved and pointed. The slabs meet at a central round disc. They are carried by a drum with fluted shafts at the eight corners. The famous round Greek *Tholoi* of Delphi and Epidaurus did not have proper domes. Their roofs consisted of straight beams rising to a central point.

by eight massive piers, without buttresses or any visible exterior resistance to break the tremendous thrust super-imposed. It is solely the niches between and hidden elliptical spaces within the piers which cunningly dissipate the load carried by arches thrown across them. These arches bring the weight down upon the concrete piers of giant strength and resistance. The support through arches constitutes the novelty and incidentally the triumph of Hadrian's engineers.[10]

The body of the Pantheon as seen today, stripped and naked and rough, is immensely satisfactory. The great sweeping cylinder is girdled by two horizontal belts or courses—the lower of five moulds—which divide it into three separate planes. Crowning it is a projecting cornice composed of those stout simple blocks which you observed from a distance, biting into the outline of the two pediments. Ghirlandaio in his *Rape of the Sabines* illustrated statuary figures standing upon the cornice against the sky, and we are told that in Roman times there stood upon the apex of the pediment a group of Jupiter in a chariot hurling thunder-bolts, and upon the lateral angles bulls, all in bronze. Today there are no such adornments. The thin Roman bricks, one and a half inches high and bedded in deep seams of mortar form but an outer skin only to the bulk of concrete behind. Here and there are the scars and fissures of nearly two millenia on the rugged surface, where patient stray cats, dirty but not starved, squat like the diminished ghosts of pagan gods enshrined within niches. A series of blind, relieving arches emphasizes the roundness and strength of the structure. The surface was originally coated with stucco and marble, of which traces are still visible around the base. There are vestiges too of a beautiful marble frieze at the rear of the rotunda on what formed part of the adjacent Baths of Agrippa. The frieze is composed of alternate honeysuckles and shells sprouting tridents, between pairs of sportive dolphins. Palladio in a woodcut of the Pantheon in his

[10] Who were they? Who was the architect? Valerius of Ostia has been mentioned, but is merely a name.

famous *Quattro Libri d'Architettura* shows the exterior surface entirely rusticated and the middle and upper stages between the courses divided by Corinthian pilasters. He was evidently depicting the outside as he thought it should have been and not as it was in the sixteenth century, for the underskin of brick and the blind arches are shown exposed in a sketch by Antonio da Sangallo, the younger, as well as in a drawing by Cronaca, both executed in the previous century.

Since a portico cannot be tacked straight on to a round building, the irregular space formed between it and the circumference is filled by a kind of vestibule (what the Greeks termed a *pronaos*). You will get an understanding of how Hadrian's architect dealt with this space by walking into the Via della Rotonda to the west of the Pantheon. From here you will see that the vestibule extends the three open side bays of the portico by two unequal-sized filled bays, making five in all. Pilasters of the vestibule are made to carry on the great entablature of the portico right up to the body of the temple. But you will observe that the adjustment was not very thoroughly carried out, for the vestibule is not properly bonded on to the rotunda and the junction of its last capital with the lower belt of the rotunda is distinctly clumsy—an accident that goes some way to substantiate the theory that Agrippa's portico was either left intact or faithfully rebuilt after the fire of A.D. 110. Both sides of the vestibule are still partly faced with a skin of marble and marble crossbands, in patterns of carved swags and ribbons.

The massive portico is octastyle, that is to say having a width of eight columns. It is the most ambitious of all the Roman porticoes and the only one to survive practically intact.[11] The more usual of the larger sized porticoes is the hexastyle (having a width of six columns) such as those of the Temples of Saturn and Concord. Here at the Pantheon are sixteen columns in three rows, of which eight are in the front and eight so disposed behind as to leave a large open

[11] In other parts of Italy decastyle and even dodecastyle porticoes of the ancients exist. But in Rome none is wider than the octastyle.

space before the central entrance and two lesser spaces before the two lateral niches of the vestibule. Thus the unusual width and depth of the portico were designed to impress the approaching visitor with its grandeur and solemnity and to suggest to him, once he had walked beneath it, the illusion of a dense forest of giant tree trunks. The central intercolumnar space of the front row obeys the Vitruvian rule in being very slightly but appreciably wider than its fellows, so as to enable a large concourse of people to enter the temple with ease. This factor does not the least detract from the symmetry of the portico and merely demonstrates the adroitness of the architect in maintaining splendidly balanced proportions.[12]

The sixteen columns are monoliths, each composed of a single block of Egyptian granite, 46½ ft high. Those in the front are grey, the rest, red. Only the three on the extreme left are seventeenth-century replacements. They are easily distinguished by the Barberini bee on the capital of the front column and the Chigi star on those of the two rear columns. All are unfluted although they are of the Corinthian order, which should be the most ornate, and according to the ancients the most delicate and feminine, of the architectural orders. The Pantheon portico is said to be the earliest example of Corinthian work in Rome. It is in fact still transitional in its immature style, which may account for the rather robust and Doric character of the columns with their deliberately accentuated swelling, implying masculinity, and the unadorned entablature which they carry. The capitals, like the bases of the columns are of Pentelic marble. This material has allowed the carving of their foliage and moulds to be unusually crisp and sharp. For the ancients knew that the quarries of Mount Pentelicus in Attica yielded the finest marble for statuary in the western world. Had not Pheidias and Praxitiles and the sculptors of the Parthenon

---

[12] A. Desgodetz points out that Palladio in his woodcut failed to make the central intercolumnar space wider than the others. This is only one inaccuracy in Palladio's illustrations of the Pantheon.

pediments and friezes put its great reputation to the proof? A comparison with Corinthian capitals of the third century A.D., such as those of the Temple of the Sun, shows the Pantheon capitals to be, not loose and naturalistic, but tightly bunched, unblown—in fact Hellenistic, a condition by no means solely induced by the unavoidable damage of centuries to the volutes and fronds. Palladio declared that their carving signified the earlier and purer Augustan century, to which he erroneously believed the whole portico to belong, and represented the leaves of the olive tree, which they certainly do not. On the contrary, the fronds resemble the narrow, spiny-toothed leaves of the plant, *acanthus spinosus*. It is true that this species of acanthus was generally favoured by the Greeks upon their capitals, whereas the broader, more deeply incised *acanthus mollis* was commonly reproduced by the Romans under the Flavian and Antonine emperors.

Palladio's assumption that the portico capitals dated from Augustus's and not Hadrian's reign would, however, be more convincing if it were not for Pliny's reference, made before Hadrian's rebuilding, to their being of Syracusan bronze, a material hardly less valuable than Pentelic marble, even when distance and cost of transport are taken into account. It is of course just possible, although unlikely that the capitals Pliny saw were the present marble ones originally gilded; and that dulled by time they appeared to him at their great height—he is known to have been short-sighted —to be made of bronze.

Upon a plain frieze, such as we usually associate with the Doric order, is the proud, clear lettering which bears testimony to Agrippa's munificence. Above it looms the high, rather ponderous and typical Roman pediment, the surface pitted with marks of the nails which formerly held in place a bronze relief of Jupiter fulminating against the rebel giants. What a contrast to the classical Greek pediment whose apex, invariably blunter than that of the Roman pediment, made the crowning feature lower, lighter and

accordingly far more serene! Whereas the Roman entablature and pediment may be as much as one third the height
of the columns which support them, those of the Greeks are
usually only one quarter.

The inside of the portico and vestibule was as I have
already indicated, designed to strike with a suitable awe
visitors to the shrine of the gods. In spite of the appalling
spoliations of Constans II and Urban VIII the bare architecture left continues to fulfil this purpose. The sense of
space is emphasized by the open roof. The giant monoliths
bear on their capitals a series of marble cross-beams which
in turn support round-headed marble arches. Upon this
superstructure wooden beams, formerly bronze plated, take
the sloping sides of the pediment. One of Serlio's drawings
shows how the original construction looked until the seventeenth century. It was based on a cantilever principle similar
to that on which steel bridges came to be designed in the
nineteenth century, with brackets to take the immoderate
strains and stresses of a weight of marble and bronze.

The wall of the vestibule is divided into three bays
occupying the entire width of the portico. Each outer bay,
measuring two intercolumns, consists of an immense niche.
In the niches once stood towering statues of the Emperor and
his friend, Agrippa,[13] for whom and by whom the original
Pantheon was raised. They are now gone, but you can see
the large nails still embedded in the naked brickwork to
which they formerly held an outer coating of marble. The
centre bay, measuring three intercolumns, is taken up by the
enormous doorway, its surrounds and entablature cut from
one piece of marble and carved with three lines of knuckle
bone motif and an outer mould of tulip heads. Serlio
observed that the surrounds were too thin in relation to the
size of the doorway, but shrewdly guessed that the architect
expressly made them so to enable the human figure to
retain some semblance of dignity in passing between them.
They enclose the original fluted bronze posts and green

[13] According to Dion Cassius, *Roman History*, Book LIII.

bronze doors, 30 ft high and studded with nail heads in the form of rosettes. Both posts and doors somehow escaped the eyes of covetous popes, although the gold with which they once were plated has long ago been stripped off. The doors were restored and some of the plates recast by the Medici Pope Pius IV in the mid-sixteenth century. Over the lintel is an open grate likewise made of bronze and still unaltered.

You will find one of the immensely solid, verdigris doorwings partially ajar, as though perpetuating the tradition that worshippers were tolerated rather than welcomed by the Roman deities, who notwithstanding their short official sojourn here have clearly never been entirely dispelled by all the benedictions of Pope Boniface and his cartloads of martyred bones. Somewhat fearfully therefore you will slink through the aperture grudgingly vouchsafed, your confidence a little perturbed by the observation that unless you are over normal height your head barely reaches the level of the doorlock. Once inside you instantly resolve that however the building may be described, it certainly is not a church. Arthur Hugh Clough sought to express this very sentiment in classical hexameters, which he deemed suitable to it:

No, great dome of Agrippa, thou are not Christian! can'st not,
Strip and replaster and daub and do what they will with thee, be so!

You will be chilled, depressed and repelled by the empty, cavernous and unspiritual vastness. Gradually as your eyes become accustomed to the twilight your courage may return and your curiosity will surely arise. Step across to the edge of the rotunda's great perimeter and lean against the fluted pilaster on your left, beside the chipped holy water stoup (probably empty) and look up. You will see above the pilaster facing you the bold projection of the great cornice of the lower stage of the rotunda. It is of Carrara marble with finely carved dentils and its frieze is of porphyry, in perfect state of preservation such as you have never beheld in an ancient building before. And it dates from the first quarter of the second century A.D. Let your eye watch it curve away from the capital of the pilaster (where it appears to meet the cornice of the attic stage under the dome) in a tremendous downward sweep like the plunge of a scenic railway, until it is momentarily broken forward over the projecting columns of the high altar, and surge away again until lost behind you. But it soon re-emerges over your head into the recess of the vestibule, where it halts against the vast marble posts of the doorway, the only undressed marble visible. This is the one place where the glorious cornice is broken. It is also the most unsatisfactory part of the interior architecture. Something seems to have gone wrong, for the cornice is allowed to cut in an ungainly fashion into the doorhead, over which appears a strikingly unclassical feature in a horse-shoe shaped arch. The confusion at this particular point is further evidence that the junction of the rotunda with the vestibule was never properly resolved.

The great Carrara cornice with its porphyry frieze con-stitutes the most beautiful and unspoilt feature of the interior. It is the belt that keeps the whole composition together. It marks the limit of comfortable height for the human eye. Every feature above it is its sequel in the immense fabric which fades away into a canopy and must surely depend upon superhuman skill for its endurance. In spite of the bold emphasis of the cornice its height from the ground is not a third that of the opening in the dome. In fact the lower stage seems somewhat independent of the rest of the interior, and you may even feel that in relation to the attic stage it is disproportionately low. Michelangelo felt something of the kind. In objecting that the ribs of the dome did not fall centrally over the columns of the lower stage, he came to believe that two different architects must have built the rotunda, the first up to the great cornice of the lower stage, and the second the attic and dome. Yet any disharmony is cleverly obviated by the part played by the lesser cornice of the attic which is so placed that its height from the ground equals the height of the summit of the dome from it. Furthermore the interior diameter of the dome is made equal to the height of the whole building from floor to summit. The exactness of these proportions is, I submit, sufficient indication that Michelangelo was mistaken, and proves the ultimate triumph of one master-mind over a few disparities.

Nevertheless you may still maintain that the proportions of the lower stage seem to be of arbitrary determination. In other words why should its height not have been made greater? Or why should not the attic stage have been made correspondingly lower, as one is accustomed to find the relative dimensions of an attic? There seems to be no reason whatever, if—and herein lies the explanation—the dome inside had been made shallower or even raised higher by means of a drum. But the whole intention of the architect was that the dome should be enormously exaggerated in depth, without being too high from the ground. His intention was governed by religious or symbolical reasons which will shortly appear. Therefore it seemed to the architect fitting that an outsized dome should rest directly upon a correspondingly outsized attic. The dome was meant to be, and is, of course, a feat of skill. It has been made expressly larger than the exterior saucer leads one to suppose. The accompanying half elevation, half section of the Pantheon fully explains what has happened and, I think, how correctly in the circumstances. You noticed that on the outside the great cylinder was divided into three stages before the saucer was reached. You will now see that the dome inside has been greatly deepened by being brought down to the level of the top of the second outer stage. Thus only two stages have been left for the wall within. These two stages have been very carefully made to coincide with their outside counterparts, not so much for the sake of architectural propriety as for reasons of structural engineering.

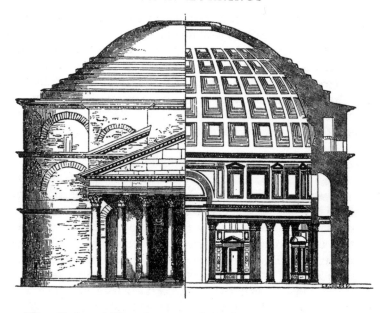

The distinguishing features of the lower stage are its eight bays, of which four are oblong recesses, two oval apses, one a semicircular apse and one the entrance. The construction and, in the main, the decoration are doubtless the original scheme of Hadrian's architect, for the columns, pilasters and entablature of the whole form a necessary sequence. Each of the four oblong recesses is composed of two fluted Corinthian columns between fluted pilasters, all of *giallo antico*, a yellow Numidian marble so rare that there was not enough to provide for the remaining bays. The theme adopted of three intercolumns, the central one wider than the others, was frequently to be copied by renaissance architects. Pietro da Cortona, for example, used it upon the lower stage of his portico of Santa Maria in Via Lata, and Bernini upon the screen before his sanctuary in Sant' Andrea al Quirinale.

Both oval apses likewise have two fluted columns between fluted pilasters—but of *pavonazetto*; the semicircular apse facing the entrance has two projecting columns of the same marble to carry the great cornice, which here follows the contour of the apse. This *pavonazetto* is not a naturally beautiful marble. Of a dirty white ground with black veins and flecks of red, it has a look of lacerated flesh. But it is fairly rare. Since it was not accounted by the Romans quite as valuable as *giallo antico*, it was dyed yellow to match the columns of the oblong recesses. Thus all the columns and pilasters of the eight bays assume a uniform dull amber tone.

Between the apses and recesses and built on to the massive concrete piers are eight little tabernacles. These familiar devices were doubtless shrines for statues of the ancestral deities, including Julius Caesar. Raised on a plinth a pair of columns support an entablature and pediment, either pointed or elliptical. The columns of two of the tabernacles are in purple granite and of another two in porphyry. Serlio would not himself have made the cornice of each tabernacle quite so high, he tells us, in relation to its architrave and frieze, yet deemed it justifiable here because of the great scale of the building. The capitals too were, he declared, made higher than Vitruvius ruled they should be in the circumstances. "Notwithstanding they are the fairest capitals that are in Rome," he conceded graciously. The tabernacles are of course the prototype of an architectural unit which has been reproduced countless times by renaissance architects for windows, embrasures and chimneypieces, of which specimens are to be found in nearly every town of Europe.[14] The decoration of the wall surface around the tabernacles has certainly been renewed, although in the original patterns. The shiny marble veneer has an impermanent thinness. The ill-fitting slabs of Brescia at the base of the tabernacles and the dingy walls of the recesses painted to feign marble probably date from Pius IX's

[14] *Vide* the windows of Peruzzi's Palazzo Albergati, Bologna, and Barry's Reform Club, Pall Mall, to take two widely distanced examples. These tabernacles (often referred to as *aedicules*) are essentially the invention of Hadrian's reign. One is to be seen in the central opening over the Arch of Hadrian in Athens.

restorations. This Pope was obliged to replace much of the broken marble and relay most of the pavement in disks of porphyry and granite and slabs of *pavonazetto* and *giallo*. Instead of sloping towards the drain in the centre of the rotunda, as you might expect, the pavement inclines towards the circumference, owing to the settled weight of the walls upon the foundation. The original floor had suffered severely from centuries of flooding. Until the Tiber embankment was formed in the last century the Pantheon was inundated with water at least once every year and on Christmas Day of 1598 to a depth of 21 ft. Nineteenth-century visitors who were punted into the rotunda at night-time affirmed that the reflection of the dome and the polychrome columns in the still waters, while moonlight filtered through the opening, was one of the most impressive sights of a Roman tour.

The present condition of the attic stage is a sad warning of the harm done by restorers when they tamper with an architect's original composition. For the decorative scheme which you see only dates from 1747. In that year the original marble face—the greatest surviving specimen of ancient polychrome decoration in the world—was scrapped and the present stucco arrangement substituted. For this act of vandalism Benedict XIV, one of the best intentioned of the rococo popes, was responsible. The wide fielded panels under wreathed strips and the pediments added to the windows (each alternate one was originally designed to shed a borrowed light from the eye of the dome into the recess below) are far too emphatic and help accentuate the scale of the attic, upon which we have already commented. To the right of the high altar, however, you may see a section of the original decoration as it was reproduced in drawings by Antonio Dosio and the cuts of Serlio and Palladio. It was on a lighter and more appropriate scale, but even so not entirely satisfactory. The openings were separated by groups of four pilasters in porphyry (their caps and bases of *giallo*) resting upon a continuous base. Between the serried pilasters were vertical and horizontal panels and circular disks of

porphyry, of Carara, isabella (a kind of buff) and serpentine
(green and scaly) marbles.[15]

The be-all and end-all of the Pantheon was of course the
dome; and there can be no doubt that it was purposely made
symbolical. Whereas the gothic cathedrals of the Christian
builders were aspirant—their pointed pinnacles and spires
reaching to the highest heaven in joyous praise of a bene-
ficent Almighty—the Pantheon was meant to be propitiatory.
Instead of striving to epitomize in stone the supreme
attributes of a single celestial god, the architect of the pagan
shrine endeavoured to devise a worldly habitat which the
elusive Roman deities might condescend to visit from time
to time. In other words the dome was meant to be a micro-
cosm of that limited universe which the Roman civilization
understood, and a kind of playground on earth for the
planetary ancestors of the imperial house, now recognized
to be semi-divine. "Pantheon, plain and round, of this our
world Majestic emblem. . . ." wrote young John Dyer in
the *Ruins of Rome*, with some insight into its purpose. The
Roman faith was after all pre-eminently anthropomorphic.
The concave dome, "seemingly suspended in the air," as
John Evelyn saw it, was the finite sky and the central
circular opening the sun, the only source of light and life,
the law-giver, the Gens Julia, round which the lesser
luminaries of the universe revolved. The Christians in taking
over the Pantheon made various uses of the opening. In the
Middle Ages when the Pope officiated in person at the
Pentecost mass, a shower of red and white rose petals was
made to descend from the aperture upon the faithful, while
a dove fluttered overhead. And again at the Feast of the
Assumption an image of Our Lady, attended by ministering
angels, was contrived to disappear through the dome in a
veil of clouds, while the congregation beneath marvelled as
much at the machinery which brought about the miracle as

[15] Pliny remarked upon the caryatides carved by Diogenes of Athens which
stood somewhere on the attic storey of the previous Pantheon and were too
high to be seen properly.

at the miracle itself. The crude and bare cement of the square sunk coffers, diminishing as they near the opening like the rays of the sun as you trace them back to their source, were of course originally covered. Serlio thought that the plaster which coated them (Inigo Jones noticed traces of plaster during his visit in 1614) had been originally plated with silver and claimed to have detected remnants of the metal. In the middle of each coffer was a bronze or gold rosette. At any rate an image of the heavens pricked with stars was clearly the intention. Today the only original decorative feature left is the bronze rim of the opening, which was spared by Urban VIII because of its necessary structural function. It is a credit to Bernini's modesty that he repeatedly declined the Pope's request that he should redecorate the dome. He assured the incredulous Urban that he had not the talent or temerity to undertake so presumptuous a task. Whereas, he exclaimed, Saint Peter's had a hundred defects, the Pantheon had not even one.

The symbolical significance of the central opening affected the construction of the dome. It made the architect's task a peculiarly difficult one. The roof instead of being vaulted had consequently to be hypaethral, i.e. open to the sky, like the vast majority of Hellenic temples. Had the small aperture been closed and the space vaulted the weight of the roof merging on a central junction could have been more evenly distributed. As it is, all the weight is borne downwards, a problem which the architect had to resolve by supporting his roof upon an elaborate series of brick corbels.

In spite of the exposed grey cement surface the dome is still a thing of much beauty, with its ranks of expanding coffers, their graduated depths chequered with shadows when the noonday sun is high. At all hours of the day the light, whatever its strength, is regularly diffused over the marble floor and walls, so that only the two cornices are strongly pencilled by darkness and the ceilings of the side chapels shrouded in twilight.

The influence of the Pantheon upon renaissance archi-
tects was of course so widespread that I need only enumerate
a few buildings which owe their derivation to it.[16] Palladio's
"Tempietto" at Maser, Bernini's Assunta at Ariccia and
Bianchi's San Francesco di Paola at Naples are three
Italian churches built within the classical revival to be
deliberately modelled upon it. Sabatini's San Francisco al
Grande in Madrid is a recognized Spanish adaptation. In
England, Henry Flitcroft's Pantheon in the gardens of
Stourhead, the anonymous Pantheon at Ince Blundell and
Decimus Burton's ineptly named and short-lived
"Colosseum" in Regent's Park were meant to be near copies
of the famous archetype. Lastly the Jefferson Monument
in Washington, U.S.A. is a twentieth-century version of the
Pantheon in glistening pink marble, with the addition of a
surrounding colonnade. In every case the embarrassment of a
central opening in the dome was overcome by the substitution
of a raised cupola. Painters on the other hand were free to
rejoice in an open dome upon perfectly flat ceilings. Rubens
in his panel of the *Union of England with Scotland* (designed at
Inigo Jones's special request) for the Banqueting House at
Whitehall depicted King James I enthroned under an open
coffered dome, the derivation of which is quite obvious.
Emanuel de Critz was in his turn inspired to contrive an
open dome in his huge ceiling oval in Inigo Jones's double
cube at Wilton. English eighteenth-century artists continued
to paint feigned hypaethral domes on the ceilings of great

---

[16] Its every feature became a model to the aspiring builder, great and small,
throughout the European classical revival. John Dyer again, in the seventeen-
thirties, exhorted him to make it his schoolroom study:

> Here, curious architect,
> If thou essay'st ambitious, to surpass
> Palladius, Angelus, or British Jones,
> On these fair walls extend the certain scale,
> And turn th' instructive compass: careful mark
> How far in hidden art the noble plan
> Extends, and where the lovely forms commence
> Of flowing sculpture; nor neglect to note
> How range the taper columns, and what weight
> Their leafy brows sustain. . . .

country houses, like the one in the saloon of Moor Park in Hertfordshire.

The influence of the Pantheon upon classical architecture of modern times has surpassed that of any building of the ancients. This was largely but by no means entirely due to the fortunate accident of its survival practically intact. Just as the Greeks revered the Parthenon as the miracle of their own civilization, so the Romans regarded the Pantheon as the supreme achievement of theirs. Nor were they unjustified in their confidence. In its feat of engineering they had outstepped their masters, the Greeks. In its dome they had carried the science of architecture a long pace forward.

BIBLIOGRAPHY

INIGO JONES. Marginal notes in his copy of Palladio's *Quattro Libri dell 'Architettura*.

A. PALLADIO. Fourth Book of *Architettura*, 1570.

G. B. PIRANESI. *Le Vedute di Roma*.

DOMENICO AMICI. *Nuova Raccolta delle Vedute . . . di Roma*, 1837.

JOHN EVELYN. *Diary*.

S. SERLIO. *Regole Generali de Architectura*, Vol. 3, 1540.

Pliny's Letters. Loeb Library.

M. ARMELLINI. *Le Chiese di Roma*, 1891

Article on the Pantheon. *The Builder*, Vol. XXI, pp. 433-4, 1863.

F. W. SHIPLEY. *Agrippa's Building Activities in Rome*, 1933.

A. DESGODETZ. *Les Edifices Antiques de Rome*, 1682.

A. BARTOLI. *I Monumenti Antichi di Roma*, 1914.

Murray's Handbook to Rome, 1899.

EARLY CHRISTIAN

———⊃∘◎∘⊂———

Santa Costanza

THE mausoleum of Santa Costanza (as its name is commonly spelt) shares with the Arch of Constantine the distinction of being the two best preserved monuments in Rome of the great Emperor's reign (A.D. 306–37). Santa Costanza can moreover claim to be one of the earliest Christian buildings to survive intact in the whole of Italy.[1]

The precise identity of the sainted lady after whom the mausoleum is named has never yet been satisfactorily established. Her conflicting stories are not without interest or bearing upon the building's history. The orthodox and generally accepted version is that the neighbouring "basilica of the holy martyr Agnes was built by the Emperor Constantine at the instance of his daughter, Constantina, likewise a baptistery [*sic*] in the same place. Here both the Emperor's sister Constantia and his daughter were baptized by Sylvester the Bishop, when the following gifts were presented, patens, chandeliers of gold and silver, etc." These words come from nothing less than the *Liber Pontificalis*, or official papal calendar, inaugurated in the sixth century, which purports to collate more or less faithfully all outstanding events in the Church's early history. A similar account had been given in the *Gesta Sanctae Agnetis* of the fifth century, wherein it was clearly stated that Constantina[2] having persuaded her father to build the basilica, "sibi illic mausoleum collocari

---

[1] It is true that the Arch of Constantine, erected in 315 to celebrate his recent victory over Maxentius bears the famous words "instinctu divinitatis" in compliment to the Emperor. They have been interpreted by some authorities as referring to his Christian faith. But the inscription read as a whole does not bear out this interpretation. The Emperor's conversion came at a later date.

[2] Henceforth, to avoid confusion, I give Constantina as the name of the Emperor's daughter, and Constantia as that of his sister.

praecepit." I must here explain that the cult of the child martyr Agnes—she was as yet uncanonized—was at this particular epoch extremely popular with Roman ladies recently converted to Christianity, since it betokened the pursuit of a virtue attractive because novel, namely chastity. In the year 304 after abortive efforts had been made to burn her alive Agnes at the tender age of thirteen cheerfully met death by decapitation rather than surrender to the lusts of young patricians in a Roman brothel.

Beyond these exiguous data the orthodox version is merely fortified by legend, which rashly claims to be more specific. It relates that one day Constantina ill with virulent scrofula was praying by the tomb of Agnes when a divine voice exclaimed "Constanter, age Constantina!" and continued "Act in the faith of Jesus Christ who will heal your disease." Immediately cured, Constantina persuaded her father to build over the martyr's tomb a basilica and close beside it a mausoleum to be her own burial place. Before this event, however, legend declares that Constantina had been betrothed by her royal father to a widowed general, Gallicanus, in reward for military services. Thereupon the general was on a sudden called away to oppose the barbarians in Thrace. On his departure Gallicanus vowed that if he were victorious he would embrace the Christian faith when he returned to claim the Emperor's daughter. He was victorious, and on his triumphant entry to Rome was greeted with the news that during his absence his betrothed had been cured of scrofula and, what was more surprising, wedded to Jesus Christ; that she had retired to a convent and also taken his two daughters to live with her as consecrated virgins. Far from displeased with this turn of events, Gallicanus seems to have accepted it as a further indication of God's all bountiful mercy. He readily renounced his betrothed, was baptized and vowed henceforth to live in continence. He devoted the rest of his days to the poor.

And now we come to the unorthodox version. Unfortunately a very different interpretation of Constantina's character is given by the Latin historian Ammianus Marcellinus. He was born about A.D. 330, so that by the time of writing, his story, it is true, already belonged to the past. But Marcellinus who was by no means intolerant of the Christian religion has never been found wanting in veracity. He was in the words of Gibbon "without the prejudices and passions which usually affect the mind of a contemporary." Yet he describes Constantina as anything but virginal and virtuous. She was first married, he declares, to King Annibalianus, the son of one of Constantine's brothers. The Emperor in making his nephew Caesar in 335 gave him the rule of Pontus, Armenia Minor and Cappadocia. The Emperor's sons on their father's death in 337 involved Annibalianus in a fairly comprehensive slaughter of their Flavian relations, and so Constantina found herself a widow. Fourteen years later she married another nephew of Constantine, called Flavius Claudius Constantius Gallus, who owing to his extreme youth had survived the pogrom of 337. He was made Caesar in 351 and sent to rule the eastern prefecture at Antioch. "To his cruelty," wrote Marcellinus, "his wife was besides a serious incentive, a woman beyond measure presumptuous. . . . She was a Megaera in mortal guise, and assiduously inflamed the savagery of Gallus, being as insatiable as he in her thirst for human blood. The pair in process of time became more expert in doing harm . . . they fastened upon innocent victims false charges of aspiring to royal power or of practising magic." Gibbon indeed called her, not a woman, but "one of the infernal furies." Finally, the then emperor, Constantius II, determined to put an end to the nefarious rulers of Antioch. First, he summoned Constantina, who was his sister, to Rome. She set out with misgivings but died on the way home of fever. Then came Gallus's turn, and he reached Italy. Asked by the Emperor why he had put so many innocent men to death Gallus replied, somewhat lamely, that he had done so at the instigation of his wife, Constantina. Enraged by this answer Constantius immediately had his brother-in-law beheaded.

This is all that Marcellinus vouchsafes us about Constantina's life and character. It is positive and damning enough. Later in his history he adds a paragraph which more or less confirms that Gallus's fury of a wife was at any rate interred in the mausoleum. After recording the death of the Empress Helena, Marcellinus continues: "The Emperor Constantius sent to Rome the remains of his deceased wife Helena to be laid to rest in his villa near the city on the via Nomentana, where also her sister [in-law], Constantia, formerly the wife of Gallus, was buried." And here I come to the end of the unorthodox version.

Now these two very divergent stories have presumably induced in your mind an extreme confusion concerning the identity of members of the imperial family, if nothing else. The confusion is caused by so many variants of the same Christian name having been given to both males and females. Constantine's three sons who on his death shared the empire were called Constantine, Constantius and Constans; his daughter was called Constantia or Constantina (in the Latin texts the name is written quite indiscriminately), and his sister Constantia also. This leads me to suggest that perhaps the Latin authors experienced the same confusion as yours and confounded the niece with the aunt. You noticed that the *Liber Pontificalis* mentioned that Constantia, the sister of the Emperor Constantine, was baptized with her niece. Since nothing to the detriment of the aunt is elsewhere recorded —Gibbon merely refers to "her pre-eminence of greatness and misery"—it may well be that she was the pious lady deserving canonization, but that owing to the tiresome similarity of name the honour fell upon her most unworthy niece.

Alas, indeed, for the reliability of the orthodox version! The posthumous *Liber Pontificalis* account, from which I have already quoted, referred to Santa Costanza having been built as a baptistery (*baptisterium*), a mistake which curiously enough the previous *Gesta Sanctae Agnetis* account did not make. Now it has been proved conclusively by recent scholars, including Professor Lanciani (indisputably the greatest Roman archaeologist of modern times) that Santa Costanza was built as a mausoleum for a Roman princess who founded a congregation of virgins at Sant' Agnese, and soon afterwards, possibly by the end of the fourth century, was turned into a baptistery to serve the basilica. They are agreed that the date of the building lies between the years 324 and 325; and that its decoration must have been completed before the leading architects and marble workers were removed by the Emperor from Rome to Constantinople in 328—for in that year there was an abrupt cessation of work in the old capital on all important buildings, among which Santa Costanza must of course be reckoned.

Like all early Christian places of worship and burial the mausoleum lies outside the City walls. Although by the fourth century the need for concealment of Christian worship was over the hygenic Roman law that burial of pagans and Christians alike must not take place within the metropolitan boundary still held good. Accordingly Santa Costanza is to be found in what was less than a century ago part of the open Campagna and is today dense suburbs. It has to be approached through the Porta Pia, Michelangelo's imposing gateway in the north-east sector of the walls of Rome, and down the ancient consular road which led to Nomentum. The Via Nomentana is a straight pre-modernistic boulevard of decent, yellow-washed buildings of the suburban sort flanking a double avenue of plane trees. After a mile and a half the entrance to the courtyard of Sant' Agnese Fuori Le Mura is reached on the left. You go through and pass on your right the splendidly ludicrous fresco depicting Pope Pius IX miraculously suspended in the air through the intervention of Our Blessed Lady, whilst braided ambassadors, empurpled cardinals and other dignitaries tumble headlong into a cellar. This reassuring incident took place during a conference when a floor on the site collapsed in the year 1854. Opposite the steps which, a little further on, descend to the basilica of Sant' Agnese you turn left and proceed down a cobbled and ramped path between walls, over which are visible the cement profiles of distant blocks of tenements. Between you and the tenements clouds of pear blossom will in spring time drift above the intervening playgrounds; in the autumn the sweet incense from smouldering olivewood is wafted to your nostrils. At the end of the path, confronting a delapidated memorial to some soldiers fallen in the defence of Rome in 1870 and an adjacent heap of Carara rubble, lies Santa Costanza. The first sight is surely unimpressive. You notice a squat pile of brickwork from which emerges an insignificant cylinder, topped by a lightning conductor and an iron cross, rusted and awry.

Practically all external embellishment was long ago stripped off the thin Roman bricks. The skeleton revealed, unlike that of the Pantheon, is undistinguished. Probably the building was never meant to make much of an exterior show. With the transition in these times from pagan temples to Christian churches ornament tended to pass from outside to inside. No longer for instance were statues of the ostentatious Roman deities enshrined on façades for the obsequious homage of passers-by. Instead the faithful were invited unobtrusively to render their private devotions to the unseen God within. Especially in circular mausoleums a change was made from the ancient external range of columns to an internal range. You notice it here at Santa Costanza in the fourth century, and at San Stefano Rotondo on the Coelian Hill in the fifth.

The front of Santa Costanza consists today of a modest brick wall with a round headed niche on either side an entrance door. Within these niches were lately found the sarcophagi of two of the princess's servitors. The doorway retains its white marble surrounds and moulded entablature whose too thin cushioned frieze is an early indication of decadence in the classical style. Flanking the front at right angles are two large hemi-cycles facing one another and bounding what Serlio described as "a walking place made in the form of an egg." It was of course originally a covered vestibule. Over the front appears another wall and sloping roof, then the cylinder, or brick rotunda pierced with arcaded windows and adorned with a belt of stone modillions.

At this stage you cannot appreciate the significance of Santa Costanza without consulting its all important plan (below). This takes the shape of a slightly reduced omega, if

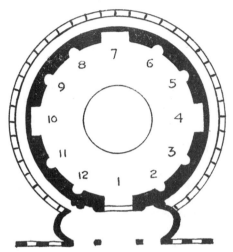

the vanished vestibule is included, or a series of concentric rings, without it. The mausoleum entrance was through the oblong vestibule, Serlio's "egg," its open side formerly marked by two columns which have now gone. The rotunda itself was surrounded by a colonnade, the outer ring, which has also gone. This colonnade had no direct communication with the closed vestibule, and only with the rotunda. What is now the recess, opposite the entrance, where the replica of the saint's sarcophagus reposes did not originally exist. In its place was an opening for access to the colonnade. The fact that the sarcophagus, in spite of the great hardness of its material, porphyry, is carved on all four faces proves that it was not originally designed for a recess. In other words it was intended for a central position, to be seen from every side. It remained for a very brief period under the arcade before the recess. The exact position is marked by an oblong slab of granite, in which are still visible round holes for the legs of the dais which upheld it. At the end of the fourth century, when the mausoleum was converted to a baptistery, the sarcophagus was removed into the arched square recess which was then formed out of the colonnade opening. At the same time a groined vault was constructed over the recess and a small lantern added to throw extra light upon the sarcophagus in its new position. On the arch soffit are the remains of thick plaster painted with eight stars in black. In the course of this change one of the window openings of the rotunda was made blind.

The great middle ring on the plan marks the existing outside wall of the circular mausoleum. It is divided transversely by the two opposing square recesses, of which I have just spoken, and two large opposing niches. In each of the four bays formed between these is a group of one lesser square recess[3] with arched head, and two lesser niches, with shelves probably meant to hold sarcophagi. These recesses and niches, unlike those of the Pantheon, fulfil no structural purpose whatever. Next comes the inner ring on the plan. It consists of twelve coupled columns carrying the drum, the thrust of which is taken by the thick outer wall and the ambulatory vault between the columns and the wall.

Here we have a landmark in the Roman architect's development of arcuated construction. The Temple of Minerva Medica, built some seventy years previously, was a step in this direction. Although a ten-sided building, and on a larger scale, its domed roof was almost but not entirely supported by ten piers between giant niches. Solid buttresses were needed as well. At Santa Costanza the architect was able to dispense with piers altogether and for the first recorded time in history supported his dome upon a series of round-headed arches on columns. It is true that at a far earlier date the Greeks had produced buildings of uninterrupted circular outline, with internal colonnades. The Tholos at Epidaurus (dating from 360–30 B.C.) is an example.

---

[3] Actually the bay to the left of the entrance now has, in place of a lesser square recess, a circular stairwell.

But the difference is that the Greek colonnades supported only a light conical roof, pierced in the centre maybe to allow the rain water to fall through, and not a solid, heavy dome. There are signs that such an occulus may have existed here.

Santa Costanza is a perfect specimen of what is called the central type of Christian architecture, wherein all emphasis is concentrated upon the hub of the edifice. The type did not develop out of the old Roman basilica plan, which, originally designed for civil uses, was a plain rectangle,[4] and when eventually adapted to Christian worship merely added a terminal apse.[5] The basilica plan is by contrast a centrifugal type of architecture, wherein men's eyes are drawn to some feature at the far end of the building. The central and centripetal type of architecture, which was derived indirectly perhaps from the familiar round temples of the ancients, existed from the earliest Christian centuries. It was employed at first solely for memorial purposes, to enshrine the tomb of a martyr or saint, and not for congregational worship. Until the fifth century the cult of saints habitually took place in the cemeteries outside the city walls. Thereafter the practice began of removing their sacred relics into churches which were then dedicated to their memories. Often an architect was faced with the more economic task of converting a mausoleum into a place of public worship by enlarging it into a basilica. This was not always easy or possible, but whenever the site allowed, the body of the church was added to the east, and the precious tomb placed there in an apse. An early example of such a transformation is Saint George at Salonika where a late third-century circular mausoleum had a choir and apse grafted on to its east end in the fifth century.

But Santa Costanza was fortunate in escaping large scale architectural transformation. It did not suffer change into a

[4] An example of an early Roman basilica is the Basilica Julia (55–44 B.C.) in the Forum Romanum, of which only the foundations remain. The best example of one partially surviving is the Basilica Maxentius (A.D. 306–12).
[5] An example of an early Christian basilica is Santa Maria Maggiore (A.D. 432–40).

basilica by the addition of a nave or choir, for the simple reason that very soon after it was built it became a baptistery. The consequent alterations were, as we have seen, inconsiderable. How long it remained in use as a baptistery is uncertain, but the *Liber Pontificalis*—in so far as it is trustworthy—tells us that by the middle of the ninth century the building was already known as the Church of Sancta Constantia. In that century the need for conventional basilican adaptation was presumably over, and no further structural alterations took place. In 1259 Santa Costanza was reconsecrated for Christian worship. Certain minor restorations were carried out and the saint's remains taken from her sarcophagus and reinterred under a central altar.

By now it is high time that you should enter the building. This unfortunately necessitates hunting for the sacristan in Sant' Agnese and exacting the key from him. Having done so, you walk straight into the circular ambulatory. The doorway under which you have to pass is of great thickness —quite five foot—and each doorpost made of a vast vertical block of undressed marble within the passageway. The jambs and the solid marble lintel which is neatly curved to follow the contour of the rotunda bear the same simple moulds as on the outside. The thickness of the whole rotunda is about twelve foot. At all seasons of the year the interior is deathly cool and still. Only the shouts of children playing around the distant tenements remind you of the life outside. As in all buildings chiefly lit from above this one is suffused with brightness. Light filters through the round headed windows of the drum and the splayed slits in the vault of the ambulatory. These nasty little openings are set at untidy intervals and the wider ones are evidently contemporary because the mosaic patterns of the vault are carefully contrived to fit round them. The floor, apart from the ring of marble under the arcades, is now covered with simple brown tiles. But in Palladio's day it was, he said, worked in mosaics—"così nel pavimento, come ne i muri e ne' volti"—of which the designs in black and white of essentially bacchic character were

recorded by renaissance artists.[6] The modern floor is desti-
tute of furnishings. Happily there is little to disturb the
architecture and decoration of the interior. And of what do
they pre-eminently consist? The inner ring of twelve arcades
and the famous mosaics of the ambulatory vault.

The four transverse arcades in front of the large recesses
and niches are made slightly wider, and accordingly slightly
higher than the remaining eight. The effect is to diversify
the pattern and reduce monotony. The result foreshadows
the familiar renaissance plan of a Greek cross within a
circle. Of the dusty coupled columns in granite two pairs in
front of the entrance and sarcophagus-recess are black and
white and two pairs red. The rest are grey. All are now dull
and rough. You may well wonder if they were not originally
kept highly polished so as to reflect the polychrome mosaics
of ceiling, floor and walls, as was customary in Roman
basilicas, whenever Corinthian and Composite columns
were purposely left unfluted, as these Composite ones are
here. Antoine Desgodetz, the French archaeologist of the
eighteenth century, discovered by his scrupulous measure-
ments that the proportions of several of the columns varied;
and it is true that the diminution of some begins at the very
bottom, of others at the top of the lowest third. All the
capitals and bases are of marble. The capitals, of which
those in the inner row are larger and fuller, are carved in
acanthus foliage resembling parsley leaves. They support a
series of unusually bold and correct entablatures, whose
comfortably cushioned friezes give great character and a
sense of ease to a splendid composition. Yet Palladio,
surprisingly enough, admired the capitals, which are really
rather coarse and inexact, and deemed the entablatures
to be imperfectly wrought and convincing evidence of
Roman decadence.

I have just stated that the building is empty of furnishings,
which is perhaps to overlook the shrine of the saint's remains.
These were enclosed, in the thirteenth century, in the marble

[6] Published in *I Monumenti Antichi di Roma*, 1914. Alfonso Bartoli.

altar-tomb set upon raised steps directly under the cupola. Behind, in the large recess stands not, alas, the original porphyry sarcophagus, but a somewhat battered replica made of plaster. According to Lanciani the sarcophagus had been violated by barbarians at a very early date and robbed of the jewels with which a Roman princess was habitually buried. The Venetian Pope Paul II was the first to move it out of the mausoleum. He placed it in the little square before his private palace of San Marco, now the Palazzo di Venezia. For four years it was exposed to injury in the Piazetta di San Marco until Sixtus IV, yielding to public clamour had it restored to Santa Costanza. There it remained for another three hundred years (apart from a brief interval when it was stolen by Paul III who intended to be buried in it) until 1788. In that year Pius VI removed it to the Vatican Gallery where it has been exhibited ever since. On the four sides of the lid portrait heads are carved. The very maidenly central head wearing ear-rings, with hair bunched on the crown (the head is duplicated on the back of the lid) is said to represent Constantina, and those on either side her father and mother.[7] But the mask of the so-called mother is surely more masculine than feminine, and therefore, if my notion that the mausoleum is Constantia's, and not Constantina's, is correct, I like to think it may really be her son's face that is here depicted (Plate facing page 30).

The design of each panel of the sarcophagus appears to be bacchic. There are scenes in relief of winged putti gathering and treading grapes while little birds peck at the vines that grow upon outsize tendrils. Interspersed among these apparently pagan insignia are a male lamb, which has been interpreted as Christ, and peacocks which are symbolic of the Resurrection.

The wall of the cylindrical drum is, like that of the ambulatory, now completely plain, with traces of nail

---

[7] Indeed on the porphyry sarcophagus of Saint Helena, now also in the Vatican Gallery, Constantine is said to have had her bust carved and that of her mother.

marks where panels in geometrical patterns, probably of marble, were formerly attached to the brick. The designs are recorded in drawings by Jacopo Sansovino. The dome of the drum is indifferently painted with scenes of the risen Christ. They were substituted under the mistaken notion of improvement after a senseless destruction of the original mosaics in 1620. Now it is no exaggeration to state that this was the worst disaster that ever befell early Christian mosaic work. Fortunately we glean some idea what the dome looked like from the rough woodcuts of Serlio and Vignola, and above all from the detailed drawings of Sansovino.[8] They all attest that the mosaics were not only of supreme historical interest, having been commissioned by the first Christian Emperor, but also among the most beautiful compositions of late Hellenistic art as yet unaffected by Byzantium. The dome, evidently meant to represent the canopy of heaven, was divided into twelve compartments by caryatids, their upraised arms reaching towards the apex, like the spokes of a wheel to its hub. The legs of the caryatids, flanked by tigers and panthers, were swathed in giant acanthus leaves and rested on rocks rising supposedly from the sea of the world that flowed uninterruptedly round the dome's perimeter. On the waters genii amused themselves in boats and on rafts, sported with swans and various aquatic birds, or fished from the shore. Within the compartments were scenes of an idyllic kind—composed of bacchantes, satyrs and humans standing and sitting in front of very realistic buildings. Several carried sacrificial animals; a few held open books. Some authorities have interpreted the scenes as purely pagan, others as Christian, even relating them to incidents in the Old and New Testaments. If Sansovino's drawings were faithful representations, then these dome mosaics may indeed have surpassed in quality those which survive on the ambulatory vault, and even have vied with the Pompeian mosaics of the early Hellenistic workers.

Although none of the mosaics of the dome is left, those of

[8] In the Library of the Escorial, near Madrid.

the ambulatory vault have been miraculously preserved almost entire. They are comprised within twelve compartments, corresponding to the twelve bays formed by the inner arcade, and are separated from each other by a kind of lightly pencilled chain border.[9] With the exception of the compartment over the entrance (No. 1 on the plan) and that over the sarcophagus recess (No. 7 and the only one deprived of its mosaics when the vault was raised and made into a groined ceiling) each is duplicated by another exactly opposite it.

No. 1 at the entrance is the simplest compartment of the lot. It was expressly made so in order to prepare the visitor for an increasing wealth of patterns as he proceeded either way under the vault towards the opening which led to the outer colonnade. It consists of Greek crosses, octagons and hexagons of black outline filled with conventional emblems in colour, on a white ground. Nos. 2 and 12 contain crosses, formed of lozenge arms, filled with chains of knuckle bones and oak leaves. In each intervening space four dolphins nuzzle at an octopus. Nos. 3 and 11 begin to show more liberal treatment. A kind of interlaced chain mould forms large and small roundels alternately. The large roundels are filled with naturalistic figures, presumably emblematic— a cloaked man with a staff, naked winged boys holding vessels, or playing on pipes, and variants of Psyche floating through the air: also storks, ducks in flight and sitting, a heron, a blackbird, a bull and a snail. The small roundels are filled with crosses made of leaves and trefoils.

Nos. 4 and 10 are above the large niches. Their pattern is still more intricate. Basically it is of flowering vines, on which boys clamber and birds peck at bunches of grapes. The composition may have inspired the vine treillage which Giovanni da Udine painted on the vault of the colonnade at the Villa Giulia. At the edges of each compartment are vintage scenes on a larger scale than that of the rest of the decoration; and in the middle a life-size bust is framed

[9] The technical name for this particular classical mould is *guilloche*.

36

among the foliage. The vintage scenes are very realistic. Wagons piled with grapes are drawn by yoked oxen led by a man with a whip.

> And the milk white oxen slow
> With the purple vintage strain
> Heaped upon the creaking wain. . . .

Slowly indeed the oxen strain, tugging their loads towards the press houses. These are rustic structures with pediments and tiled roofs. Within them men, naked but for loin cloths, are jubilantly treading the grapes, from which the juice gushes into vats beneath. The men have black curly hair, almond shaped eyes and muscular limbs. They wield flails and sticks, and one eats a bunch of grapes as he dances. The pair of busts are among the best Roman portraits of the period. Owing to their prominent positions in the two central compartments we suppose them to represent important personages associated with the mausoleum. But whom? Since they are busts of a woman and a man the adherents of the unorthodox version have concluded that they represent Constantina and her husband, Gallus. And it is true, the male bust (No. 4) somewhat resembles the effigy of Gallus found on his coins. Here the morose face is of a youth—and Gallus died tragically in his thirtieth year. He wears no beard, but his hair is fair and long. The features are distinctly handsome. And Marcellinus describes how Gallus, with his soft golden hair, had great dignity and beauty. Here the figure wears no diadem, but a shirt sewn with gold, which was reserved for Caesars in the third and fourth centuries. The female bust (No. 10) represents a sitter of mature age, and since the terrible Constantina had been married to her first husband, Annabalianus, twenty years before she became the wife of Gallus in 351, she was of course greatly his senior in years. Here the face with downward drooping mouth is extremely pensive, and the expression, it cannot be denied, is both proud and dejected. The hair is gathered with a clasp in the way in which early fourth century medals depict the coiffure of ladies of the imperial family.

These plausible conjectures are, however, instantly set at naught by our recollecting that the mosaic decoration of Santa Costanza dates before 328. Therefore the portrait of Gallus, who was not married to Constantina until 351, can certainly be ruled out. That of Annibalianus could perhaps be substituted if the female bust were of a young woman, which Constantina was at the time of his death. On the other hand, what evidence is there to contradict the supposition that the female bust represents her aunt, the Constantia pre-eminent for her greatness and misery? If the supposition is acceptable, then the male bust may be that of her only son, Licinius, who was made Caesar and finally murdered with his cousins in the Flavian pogrom. By 328, Licinius, to whom his mother was devotedly attached, was still a very young man.

Nos. 5 and 9 contain medallions, mostly of busts of youths, erased (to use a heraldic term) at the chests, and conventional flower-heads. Numbers 6 and 8 are the most beautiful compartments of all, in spite of the fact that they show absolutely no attempt at design. In accepting a complete abandon of all artistic principle you are left to face an indiscriminate medley of naturalistic forms which somehow compose a tapestry of extraordinary charm. And tapestry is the right word because the nearest familiar comparison with these two mosaics is the luxuriant verdure panels which the French factory at Fontainebleau wove in the early sixteenth century. Yet never did the Fontainebleau panels, now after a bare four hundred years mostly toned to dusky hues, display the brilliant and glowing colours which these mosaics have retained untarnished throughout sixteen centuries. When the shafts of morning sun stream through the uncouth openings in the vault, then the colours assume a dewy freshness as though the cubes of mosaic have just been inserted. Against a white ground are thrown helter-skelter, wherever space has allowed, laden branches of orange, lemon and pomegranate, among which birds, whose huge scale is quite unrelated to the fruit, mate, perch and pick their way. There are a pheasant, partridge, peacock and mallard. Other curiosities include a large conch and a cockle-shell, an amphora, a horn with gold bands and a sling, a bowl, a hand-mirror, a sheaf of wheat, a lute and a jug.

Although with two exceptions the design of each compartment of the ambulatory vault is duplicated, there is a subtle distinction in the quality of the work between the compartments on either side of the mausoleum. In other words compartments Nos. 2–6 are noticeably less refined in technique and less artistic in design than the corresponding compartments, Nos. 8–12. For example, the four dolphins nuzzling at an octopus in No. 2 are more uncouth in outline and clumsier in action than they become in No. 12. The delightful selection of brightly coloured emblems in No. 6 are far more crowded than they are in No. 8. Finally, the two vintage scenes in No. 4 are infinitely inferior to those in No. 10. In No. 4 both scenes are exactly the same, whereas in No. 10 they are noticeably individual. The one is clearly intended to represent *Morning*, for the reluctant oxen have to be cajoled and whipped by the drivers as they set forth on the day's work; the other evidently represents *Evening*, for here the oxen jog contentedly and willingly homeward. Our inference must therefore surely be that the artist began the mosaics at the entrance vault and steadily worked his way round from right to left, improving as he proceeded.

Within the heads of the two large lateral niches, are the remains—for whatever their origin they have been much restored—of compositions entirely different to the geometrical patterns of the circular vault. They are pictorial mosaics, now generally considered inferior works of the fifth or even seventh centuries, but attributed by Florian Jubaru[10] to the end of the fourth century when the rotunda was made into a baptistery. In the right niche (bay No. 4 on the plan)

[10] Florian Jubaru—*La Decorazione Bacchica del Mausoleo di Santa Costanza —L'Arte*, 1904.

Christ is delivering the keys of heaven to Saint Peter. He is seated on a globe and is bearded and haloed. He wears a green and purple mantle with an orange border. Saint Peter in a white robe stretches across the water to Him. There are two palm trees next to Saint Peter and seven, symbolical of the land of Judaea, on the other side. In the left niche (No. 10) Christ stands on a mount between Saint Philip and Saint Thomas, to whom he addresses the words "Dominus pacem dat," inscribed on a scroll beside the Signum Labarum. Over the head of Christ is a crude little cross in black set askew. In the background are again two palm trees with curious telescopic trunks, two huts and, in the foreground, four lambs representing the faithful. The lambs are disposed in pairs on either side of the sources of the three rivers of Paradise. The whole scene is framed within deep borders of pomegranates and grapes, very naturalistic. They were adapted by Giovanni da Udine for his famous garlands that adorn the gallery ceiling of the Villa Farnesina.

If Jubaru's conjecture were right—and the concensus of contemporary archaeological opinion is against him—then the mosaics of the two niches in Santa Costanza would rank with that of Christ and the Apostles in the apse of Santa Pudenziana as the earliest religious groups in Christian mosaic work. They would even anticipate Sixtus I's famous and far more accomplished Testament scenes in Santa Maria Maggiore. The truth probably is that Jubaru was correct in supposing the mosaics of the right niche to date from the fourth century, but wrong as regards those of the left. The restoration of both niches makes it difficult to date the mosaics from technical or even stylistic evidence: but enough remains of the original figures to allow a general deduction to be made from the character of the heads alone. In the right niche Christ is represented as a middle-aged man and Saint Peter as a youth. These relative ages of the Son and an Apostle were usual in figurative art of the earliest Christian era, but they were of very short duration. In the left niche a complete transformation has occurred: Christ has become comparatively youthful and the two Apostles

old greybeards in accordance with the conventional symbolism that was to last for centuries.[11] Furthermore the
grouping of the figures in the left niche is less hesitant and
more assured than in the other. They must therefore belong
to a later date.

The geometrical compartments of the ambulatory vault
are certainly the earliest Christian mosaics of whatever kind
in existence. They are also the last examples of classical
mosaics before the Byzantine influence was felt in Rome in
the fifth century. Whereas they lack the perfect refinement
of the best work in this medium executed in the great houses
of Pompeii three centuries previously, they nevertheless
surpass the crude attempts made contemporaneously at
idealization of the godhead and the saints, such as that in the
right niche depicting Christ and Saint Peter. They belong
to a period transitional from purely decorative to didactic
art. They were composed by an artist who was not afraid of
copying the out-of-date decorative motifs largely used in
stucco upon the vaults of subterranean basilicas and tombs
in the two preceding centuries, and who had not yet grasped
the revived technique of realistic portraiture which was to
develop in the ensuing Byzantine centuries.

It is true that the surviving vault mosaics at Santa
Costanza may show little positive evidence of Christian
symbolism; but it is there none the less. If you look carefully
you will see in the vault compartments 6 and 8, and again
in No. 11 (within a roundel of Psyche) several insignificant
little crosses. They bear absolutely no relation to the patterns
of the compartments, but appear mysteriously and timor-
ously, like afterthoughts. On the whole, however, the
patterns and emblems seem to you still frankly pagan. The
cheerful vintage scenes led renaissance artists like Serlio to
believe the mausoleum had been built as a temple to
Bacchus. But they overlooked the fact that in the very early
centuries pagan symbolism had to be adopted by Christian

[11] The invariable exception was Saint John, the beloved disciple, always
represented as a youth.

artists, for the obvious reason that as yet no other had been
established. The repeated use of trailing grape foliage may
have meant tentatively to symbolize the True Vine or
Eucharistic Sacrament. The constant image of Psyche may
have signified the passage of the human soul in its search for
the eternal rewards of the Christian heaven. These very
motifs, of undoubted pagan origin, were adopted with
unmistakable meaning on mosaic pavements of the African
colonies in still later centuries. Furthermore some of the so-
called Bacchic scenes appear upon the contemporary
sarcophagus of Santa Costanza herself. The explanation
clearly is that the early Christians were not forbidden to use
pagan motifs. They naturally interpreted the mysteries of
their new faith in the only traditional terms to which they
were accustomed. After all a great deal of the Catholic
symbolism, which we take for granted today, is of pagan
derivation. Altar candles, lamps before images, incense and
holy water stoups were used in the temples of the ancients.
The *porta santa* of each basilican church in Rome, exclusively
reserved for the Pope to pass through in Jubilee years, has
its source in the *porta triumphalis*, which was only opened for
the entry of a victor to the Capitol. The Scala Santa, climbed
by the faithful on their knees, correspond to the sacred stairs
of the Clivus Capitolinus, which were reverently mounted
by Julius Caesar in the same manner. Even the nimbus
which around the head of Christ and the saints indicates
extreme sanctity was put behind the head of a Roman
leader to denote power. Finally, Saint Augustine[12] tells us
that it was customary for early Christian mourners to visit
the tombs of the martyrs cup in hand, to make libations and
indeed to dance over the remains of the deceased in a state
of wildly joyous, but not disrespectful inebriation. A more
Bacchic practice than this can hardly be imagined.

[12] *Saint Augustine's Confessions*, VI. 2.

BIBLIOGRAPHY

J. G. DAVIES. *Origin and Development of Early Christian Church Architecture*, 1952.

AMMIANUS MARCELLINUS. *History of the Roman Empire*, Loeb Library.

A. PALLADIO. Fourth Book of *Architettura*, 1570.

M. ARMELLINI. *Le Chiese di Roma*, 1891.

S. SERLIO. *Regole Generali de Architectura*, Vol. 3, 1540.

H. BARBET DE JOUY. *Mosaiques Chrétiennes*, 1857.

FLORIAN JUBARU. *La Decorazione Bacchica del Mausoleo Di S. Costanza, L'Arte*, 1904.

J. P. RICHTER and A. CAMERON TAYLOR. *Golden Age of Classic Christian Art*, 1904.

C. A. CUMMINGS. *A History of Architecture in Italy*, 1901.

A. L. FROTHINGHAM. *Monuments of Christian Rome*, 1908.

ADRIEN BLANCHET. *La Mosaique*, 1928.

KARL LEHMANN. The Dome of Heaven, *Art Bulletin* XXVII, 1954.

ROMANESQUE

———◦◉◦———

Santa Maria in Cosmedin

THE equivocal Early Christian style of architecture, which lasted but a few centuries, is barely distinguishable from the late Roman. It soon evolved into the more positive Romanesque style which in Italy was to endure for a whole millenium. This Romanesque style was the outcome of two conflicting geographical influences: the political and social ideals of west and east, of the old abandoned capital of Rome and the newly founded metropolis of Constantinople. In the composite style which resulted the Roman influence, notwithstanding the political weakness of the western Empire and rather because of the counterpoise of papal ascendancy, held its own and predominated.

One of the most remarkable things about mediaeval architecture in Rome was its almost complete resistance to Gothic elements. This is the more strange when one recollects that the Gothic style is wholly derivative from Catholicism, of which the fount and seat was Rome itself. In this great city there is scarcely a building that can be described as integrally Gothic, if the thirteenth century interior of Santa Maria sopra Minerva be excepted. And in terms of the cathedrals of, say, Milan, Beauvais, Segovia and Lincoln, how pathetically wretched is that church's attempt at the pointed arch and vault. In other words mediaeval Rome never entirely forgot or forsook her ancient classical history in spite of past centuries of strife with barbarian invaders from the north. Though these people were unable to contribute anything in the way of art or architecture to the vanquished Roman Empire, it would be a mistake to assume that they necessarily devastated what the Romans had built in their heyday. On the contrary the early German tribes were

The Pantheon

Left Santa Costanza – a
compartment of the
mosaic Ambulatory
ceiling
Below left Santa Costanza –
view of the Ambulatory

Right Santa Maria in
Cosmedin
Below Santa Maria in
Cosmedin – the Bishop's
marble chair

remarkably respectful towards the ancient monuments, which they held in a sort of superstitious reverence. Alaric, King of the Visigoths having entered Rome, pillaged her art treasures it is true, but purposely refrained from damaging the public buildings; Genseric the Vandal carried off whatever articles of value had been left over by Alaric but let the monuments remain intact; and Theodoric, King of the Ostrogoths, went so far as to repair the aqueducts and even organized bands of watchmen whose duty it was by day and night to protect the statues and preserve the antiquities of the city. What is more, these measures were taken by the barbarian king not against his own disciplined hordes but against the Romans themselves, for by the fifth century the citizens, Christian and pagan alike, had become the greatest menace of Rome's past splendours, the first through fanatical revenge, and the second through apathy. The Christians who regarded the ancient monuments as symbols of their oppression and of paganism were the worse iconoclasts. Converts like Saint Augustine positively encouraged their destruction which they hailed as the just retribution of Jehovah. Pope Gregory the Great in a later century treated them with the same pious aversion. The pagans, broken by a chain of disasters and without the consolation of a new creed were utterly indifferent to the fate of the monuments and allowed them to be broken up as rubble. The attitude of the Emperor Honorius was typical of the tired but proud Roman patrician who could not yet bring himself to embrace the Christian religion and worship the god of the plebs. When the news was brought to him at Ravenna by his chamberlain that Rome was captured— this was in 410—the Emperor was at first surprisingly dejected. "Why!" he exclaimed, "She was feeding out of my hand only an hour ago." When informed that it was not his favourite hen (to which he had given the name of Roma) but merely the capital of the ancient world which had fallen, Honorius soundly rated the chamberlain for giving him an unpleasant shock.

San Pietro in Montorio

In the middle ages the city was still so rich in classical remains, in columns, entablatures, capitals and marble details of all sorts, legacies overlooked or spared by the succession of depredations made on classical monuments throughout the dark ages, that there was little need for builders to tax their creative powers.[1] Through the long millenium there was very little new architecture at all, and constant alteration and adaptation of old buildings. In Rome dwellings and churches simply evolved out of ancient classical monuments. Noble families like the Caetani and Frangipani, for example, made themselves fortresses out of what survived of the tomb of Cecilia Metella and the Arch of Titus, treated by previous centuries as mere quarries of stone and marble. Popes and religious Orders turned pagan temples and public exchanges into Christian churches with the minimum amount of trouble and cost. Successive generations altered and reedified them to suit the almost imperceptible changes in use, fashion and taste, but seldom positively pulled them down. This practice continued until the Renaissance, when Italian confidence was again restored and quantities of new buildings arose from the foundations upwards in an altogether new style. The story of Santa Maria in Cosmedin is that of a church begun, re-begun and continued intermittently throughout the course of the Middle Ages. Since its very judicious restoration over half a century ago it is probably less obviously affected by renaissance and baroque alterations than any other mediaeval structure of importance left in Rome.

Santa Maria in Cosmedin stands in the Forum Boarium and dominates a south-west corner of the ancient city on the left bank of the Tiber. The neighbourhood was and still is densely packed with Roman monuments of every date.

---

[1] Professor Lanciani disputed this cause and quoted other Italian sites equally rich in classical remains, like Pisa and Orvieto where Gothic buildings arose. He attributed the cause to mediaeval Rome never having enjoyed any form of municipal self-government and all building consequently being restricted to the church and nobility. But this argument implies that all the mediaeval popes and princes were necessarily reactionary in their artistic patronage, and is clearly not true.

Between the church and the river, where the Cloaca Maxima discharged its refuse, are the Republican rectangular Temple of Fortuna Virilis and the Augustan round Temple of Mater Matuta. Only a few yards to the north of it are the remains of the Gate of Septimius Severus and the Arch of Janus Quadrifons, dating from the third and fourth centuries respectively. Indeed the church itself arose out of, and still incorporates fragments of, the Statio Annonae, or grain market, which was erected in the fourth century in the shadow of a then existing temple to Ceres. The association with corn was maintained long after the transformation of the pagan secular building to a Christian conventicle in the sixth century, for the original conventicle was no more than a simple hall constructed within the corn market and just large enough to hold a small congregation. Later the hall was turned into a presbytery reserved for the clergy, the congregation during masses being obliged for lack of room, to stand out of doors, maybe under an awning. The place became one of the diaconal centres set up in each parish, whence corn with other necessaries continued to be dispensed to the poor, the sick and needy pilgrims. Among the last there drifted throughout the eighth century an ever mounting stream of Greek artists fleeing from the iconoclastic persecutions of the Byzantine emperors who were bent upon stopping the worship of images. Not only were works of art in the churches of Byzantium destroyed wholesale but their creators, frequently deprived of hands and arms were exiled. To Rome, which had persistently condemned the iconoclasts, they turned in desperate quest of livelihood. The wretched artists crowded on to the boats of the Sicilian merchants trading between Byzantium and the Tiber, where they disembarked. They tended to gather round the diaconal hall in the Forum Boarium, at first for physical relief, then for spiritual succour and later for the education of their children. Thereupon a Greek colony sprang up in the Forum and in time the conventicle assumed the title of Santa Maria in Schola Graeca. By 782 the converted granary proved no longer adequate for the requirements of a growing parish of foreigners and was accordingly enlarged and improved.

The person who foresaw the need for improvements and made himself responsible for carrying them out was the Colonna Pope Adrian I. This splendid scion of one of Rome's most historic families was the greatest protector of her monuments and the most enthusiastic promoter of works of art since Pope Damasus in the fourth century. Adrian first set about removing the decayed remains of the Temple of Ceres which overhung and seriously threatened the safety of the hall. Then he proceeded to make of the hall a church. He extended it towards the east into a nave, added two aisles, formed a crypt and built a portico and porch. As a concession to the Greek custom that men and women worshipped separately, Adrian provided a women's gallery, over the aisles.[2] His principal architect, Januarius, who directed most of the papal building of this reign, superintended the work. The embellishments in marble and fresco, largely carried out by the immigrant Greek artists were so much appreciated that the name of the building became changed to that of Santa Maria in Cosmedin (from κοσμειν, meaning to adorn).[3] By now it was fully a church in the traditional basilican form, a worthy monument to an enlightened pope, whose reign happily coincided with an interval of peace and a return of prosperity to Italy after the extinction of the last of the Lombard invaders in 774.

The form of the church which stands today is basically as Pope Adrian determined it. By the eighth century churches had assumed a recognizably conventional form. The early Christian basilica always had its longer axis placed east and west but the priest in celebrating mass habitually faced his congregation over the altar, thus looking towards the east. The entrance was accordingly at the east end. But in the

[2] Women's galleries survive in the basilica of Sant' Agnese and in Santa Maria in Domnica.
[3] Siric, Archbishop of Canterbury as late as 990 referred to it as Santa Maria in Schola Graeca.

fifth century the priest tended to turn his back on the congregation while still facing the east. Consequently the position of the main entrance and altar changed places and Adrian naturally planned his church according to what was then accepted practice. There is one thing he did which has, however, no precedent in western Europe and never became popular in Rome. He gave to the east end a triple apse according to the Byzantine tradition. It is easy to understand the reason why. A single apse to a nave is commonly found in Roman churches, but Adrian ended his aisles in the same fashion. He then had them covered with frescoes by the Greek artists.

Since Pope Adrian's reign several structural alterations to Santa Maria in Cosmedin have taken place. In the eighth century much damage was done to the church by an earthquake. Repairs were carried out by Pope Saint Nicholas I, who took the opportunity of adding a sacristy and oratory to the south-west. The last important changes were undertaken at the beginning of the twelfth century under the pontificate of Gelasius II (1118–19) and continued under that of his successor Callixtus II, who had previously been the church's Cardinal Deacon. The changes coincided with a period of renewed church building activity consequent upon the far-reaching liturgical reforms of Hildebrand. The man directly responsible for the changes was the Papal Chancellor Alfanus, then Cardinal Deacon of Santa Maria. Briefly, his work consisted in raising the floor of the interior, substituting round-headed arches for flat architraves in the aisle arcades, removing the women's gallery which was no longer needed, constructing the *schola cantorum*, adding the baptistery to the north-west and the campanile to the south-west, and reconstructing the portico. Santa Maria in Cosmedin, as we recognize it today, was ready for consecration on 6th May, 1123, on which occasion the date was cut on the table of the high altar.

Nineteenth-century guide books speak of the disgracefully ugly modern front of this church. In fact it was not very ugly but its presence was unfortunate. It was a fairly common-place baroque façade, having an enlarged central window under a heavy raised cornice with ramps curving downward from nave to aisles. It was imposed upon the mediaeval front in 1718 by Cardinal Albani, the patron of Winckelmann and great collector of antiquities, who considered himself the beautifier of a structure hitherto unworthy of notice. Between 1894 and 1899 it was removed amid the acclamation of all good antiquaries. In those years the church was most judiciously restored to the mediaeval condition in which Alfanus left it. Since so many of the early churches in Rome have been overlaid with indifferent baroque trappings the restoration of Santa Maria in Cosmedin, one of the least spoilt apart from its façade, was surely justified. The front now revealed is extremely un-assuming and discreet. All that can be seen of it is three round-headed windows and the top of the nave, of bare brick but originally, no doubt, adorned with fresco or mosaic. The rest of the front is concealed by the portico, which crosses the whole width of the church, and the porch. The remaining three sides of the church are encrusted with small mean dwellings, in the true mediaeval tradition. It is doubtful whether these elevations were ever meant to be seen. Out of the body of the church surges the tallest of the *campanili* on the Aventine and the most spectacular of those which survive in Rome.

In every apparent sense Romanesque in style the square *campanili* of Rome are nevertheless a legacy from the Lombards. These barbaric people when they swept down from the north were impressed by the solitary round towers which everywhere they saw punctuating the Italian land-scape. A few of these towers still stand at Ravenna detached from the churches which they served. The Lombards felt impelled by some odd instinct to emulate them. But they did not build their own towers on a round plan. They built them square. At first they made them severely plain; later they adorned them with pilaster strips and engaged shafts, and provided arched openings which increased in number towards the summit. For many centuries the Lombard towers were built to an unvarying pattern, and the oldest as well as the greatest number have curiously enough survived in Rome—which the invaders never succeeded in capturing. Alfanus's *campanile*, which is square on the Lombard plan, consists of seven visible stages of round-headed openings separated by cornices with pronounced modillions. Two further stages of the base, which are hidden, may even be part of Pope Adrian's constructions.

Alfanus's reconstructed portico can only be entered through Adrian's central porch, properly called a *propylon*. This appendix to a basilica was completely unknown to the Romans and only used by the Greeks in a highly refined form as the entrance to their most important acropolises. Here it has declined into a kind of debased hood with a shouldered and rounded arch sustained by four Ionic columns, of which the two inner are of fluted marble and rest on no bases. Two of the capitals are late Roman; two are clearly mediaeval. The coeval *propylon* at San Clemente closely resembles the one here. Others of later date and more sophisticated design are to be seen in front of several Romanesque churches in Provençe.

The portico suffered a good deal of alteration outside when Cardinal Albani's baroque front encased it with elegant Corinthian pilasters made to support a heavy entablature and attic. In stripping these adjuncts, the restoration has left it absolutely simple, doubtless far more so than when Alfanus had finished with it. The naked bricks are of the Roman one and a half inch height. The seven bays stretch the full width of the nave and aisles. All have been given grills. Normally the mediaeval porticoes had flat lintels and not round-headed openings, as you will find in the far better preserved porticoes of San Giorgio in Velabro, a stone's throw away, and of San Lorenzo fuori le Mura. Possibly therefore Pope Adrian's original portico partook of this character before his successor reconstructed it in the twelfth century and added a storey lit by narrow windows over the arcades.

The vaulting of the portico is essentially plain. Against the north end of the arcade rests in an upright position the fabulous marble disk, the *"Bocca della Verità,"* from which the church now derives an alternative title. It is a Roman drain head representing the mask of Oceanus, or even Tiber, through whose open mouth, round eyes and dilated nostrils once seeped the rain water and ordure of a past civilization on its way to the Cloaca Maxima. In the middle ages the drain head attracted superstitious reverence and judges came to believe that the hand of a suspected witness put through the mouth would be bitten if he committed perjury. Augustus Hare relates how in the last century an incredulous Englishman was persuaded to put in his hand and tell a lie, and was promptly bitten by a scorpion. The esteem in which this mask is held by the public may be gauged by the number of names, scratched, chalked and written with indelible ink upon it since the war. The forlorn features, the puckered brow and faintly pencilled locks are in consequence practically obliterated. The desecration of Roman monuments by visitors within the past ten years cannot be paralleled with that of the previous ten centuries from the same cause. Such conduct is after all but one of the consequences of democratic self-expression.

Built against the nave wall to the right of the main entrance is the canopied alabaster tomb of Cardinal Alfanus who died in 1150. A clumsy pediment is carried by foliated Gothic caps upon thin shafts. The strips between the panels of the tomb-table are of Romanesque character. On the table a cross sprouting from a skull has been rudely carved by a visitor of many centuries ago. A touching Latin inscription records that "Vir probus Alfanus cernens qua cuncta perirent hoc sibi sarcofagum statuit ne totus obiret. . . ."—Alfanus a man of probity, in recognizing that all things must perish, nevertheless had this memorial to himself erected so that he might not die absolutely. The central doorway combines such a medley of styles, of decorative and symbolical motifs, that its date cannot precisely be determined. It was wrought by one Iohannes de Venetia either for Pope Adrian or Pope Callixtus. Its moulds are a compromise between classical and Gothic patterns. On the face of the jambs a parade of uncouth dentils, honeysuckles, egg and tongue knucklebones is a reminder of the old Roman regard for conformity and order. On the lintel and within the jambs a flowing tracery vividly denotes the mediaeval love of meandering ease. In its foliage are interspersed crosses, a bear, a hedgehog, a fish, a squirrel and a fox with a waving brush. On the under surface is an emblem of God the Father, a right hand with fourth finger crooked in the act of blessing you as you pass underneath. At either end are the Lion of Saint Mark, two rams, a pair of doves, each feeding from a vase and a third perching upon a dragon to signify the victory of the purified soul over worldly temptations. Over the doorhead totter three rusty tin shields bearing the papal arms.

The interior of Santa Maria in Cosmedin today gives you a very faithful idea how one of the larger mediaeval churches originally looked. It is a better archetype than the neighbouring San Giorgio in Velabro with its air of timeless seclusion, but empty and unadorned: than San Clemente, richer far in works of art but lacking true mediaeval character because overlaid by a ponderous baroque ceiling: than the basilica of San Lorenzo, now restored after terrible damage by bombs in 1943. It is comparatively unspoilt, bare of all extraneous furnishings, severe, uncouth, uncompromisingly mediaeval. The relief it offers after the relentless roar of motor traffic over the cobbles outside is heavenly indeed. On entry you step down quite literally, into the refreshing austerity of the twelfth century. The chill air is rinsed in that charnel smell of must and damp which is inseparable from all mediaeval Catholic churches on the Continent, and which

the initiated church-roamer learns to recognize and grows
to love. It is the breath of his being, this effluvium of stale
incense, bones, decaying parchment and sacramental oil.
In early spring, when Rome is at its most deserted and most
promising, and at an hour when Mass is over, you will for
the greater part of the morning be the sole visitor, left to
your own devices once you have satisfied the small boy with
a shaven head and aloe eyes, dressed in an alpaca jacket of
ankle length, who collects tribute to the maintenance fund
either of the church or himself. Whatever the cause, be sure
to give something. Only occasionally will the screaming door
open to let in a momentary gale of traffic din and maybe
a hesitant Scandinavian art student, who is very soon
oppressed by the loneliness of his own footsteps, and stealthily
withdraws.

Having recovered from the first shock of arrested time you
notice two things, firstly the glimmer of returning warmth
engendered by the multi-coloured floor and, secondly, the
extreme oddness of the church's shape. The last was not at
all apparent to you from the outside, for Roman church
façades never betray the slightest hint of what you may find
within. Their inscrutability is one of their teasing habits. A
glance at the plan confirms that Santa Maria in Cosmedin,
far from being a regular rectangle has none of its four sides
parallel and that midway up the nave the body of the
seeming rectangle takes a slight bend to the right like a
broken stick. In short, the more you study the plan the more
you discover anomalies. Regard for right angles appears to
have been based on guesswork for lines are made to converge
and then dart off at tangents. The left aisle is perceptibly
wider than the right and narrows towards the east. The
nave is splayed at its west end, and the right aisle at both its
ends. The sacristy is deliberately shaped like a trapezium
and everywhere walls thicken and diminish at will. Moreover
the three apses do not correspond in any particular. In other
words you derive from this church a very sound understanding of the meaning of a mediaeval building which is

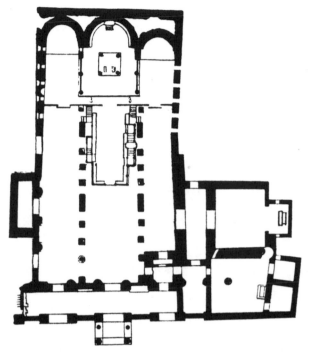

not truly Roman, Lombard or Byzantine, but is a protracted evolution of all three styles.

The extraordinary muddle is to some extent explained by the eleven gigantic Roman columns still visible, embedded in the walls of the church. These, which are fluted and have Corinthian capitals, are remains of the fourth century Statio Annonae. Their disposition shows that the Roman grain market was sited from north to south across what is now the west half of the existing church. The three columns seen in the north aisle wall formed part of the vestibule of the Roman building. The two equal spaces between them are wider than any of the spaces between the seven remaining columns of the long west elevation. Of these seven columns, all in a straight line, three are to be seen in the west wall of the church, one in the base of the campanile, two in the space between the campanile and the sacristy and one in the sacristy. The eleventh and last of the visible columns stands in the wall between the sacristy and Lady Chapel and to the east of the line of seven. The returned position of this last column seems to indicate the limit of the plan of the grain market. I write "seems to indicate" because the seven columns in straight line are not equispaced, and so cannot all be precisely on their original sites.

The nave of the church is separated from the aisles by the round-headed arcades on a variety of columns, of which eighteen are antique. None of them agree with their capitals, which are mostly Romanesque. Five of the capitals date from the time of Pope Adrian and the pair facing each other, the second in each row, are Byzantine with carved naked figures of much delicacy and feeling. Nearly all have been ruthlessly chopped about and one Composite capital next to the Gospel pulpit has not even been set straight upon its shaft. The walls carried by the arcades are plain, coated with a dirty distempered plaster, occasionally exposing traces of rubble. Around the small clerestory windows are obscure remains of mediaeval paintings. The flat nave ceiling which dates from the late seventeenth century was painted a celestial grey, now worn to brown, and sprinkled with white stars after a fashion common in Pope Gelasius's time. It may therefore be an exact replacement of what existed originally.

Inset in the wall of the west end, on either side of the main door, are two purply-black stone objects, of the size and shape of Dutch cheeses, but of the colour and texture of an aubergine. They are Roman standard weights, relics of the old grain market and according to tradition used in times of persecution to stone the martyrs. On either side of the organ loft are Byzantine lunettes, or rather heads of those windows uncovered on the outside when Cardinal Albani's baroque façade was stripped off. They are filled with circles and half circles of milled outline, and are now glazed. These

Byzantine openings are repeated in the three apses of the east end. Originally the circles and half circles were filled either with slabs of opaque, colourless marble, perforated to let in the light, or with translucent alabaster.[4] Stained glass was as yet unknown—it was seldom adopted in Roman churches and is rather a northern and Gothic form of embellishment— and colour was sought not so much from above as from below. It was concentrated upon floors. And the floor of the nave and aisles of Santa Maria in Cosmedin was laid for Cardinal Alfanus in 1123.

It is a very conspicuous feature of the church. Like an enormous, evenly spread oriental carpet in geometrical patterns of squares and circles interlaced, it throws up the warmth and colour so much needed. Grey, purple, green, red, yellow and blue are the colours that predominate, and in the middle like a pool of wine is splashed a vast circle of porphyry. *Opus musivum* the guide books call this paving grandiloquently, or even *opus alexandrinum*. But the first term merely means mosaic work confined to pavements, and the second denotes the traditional pattern form of circles and scrolls used in Rome ever since the Emperor Alexander Severus made it popular early in the third century[5]. Its earliest form consisted of pebbles aimlessly stuck in a concrete ground. Gradually as greater attention was paid to materials, multi-coloured marble chips were chosen. Then patterns emerged. Until the thirteenth century Roman churches vied with one another in the splendour of their floor mosaics, which, however, never attained the same refinement as wall mosaics. Often the first were paid for by the poorer members of a congregation, whereas the second were supplied by rich princes and nobles.

The practice of this particular style of mediaeval mosaic work became the exclusive profession of certain families settled in Rome, often wrongly classified as one family, and

---

[4] Many windows of Orthodox churches in the island of Rhodes are still filled with translucent alabaster.

[5] Pavements in *opus alexandrinum* are easily distinguishable from early pagan pavements, which were usually in pictorial patterns, and of finer workmanship.

called the Cosmati. Nevertheless, for convenience sake, we may speak of the Roman marble workers of this period as the Cosmati school. Members of the school did not confine their work to pavements and walls. They also designed and made tombs, pulpits, paschal candlesticks and choir screens, which they spangled with mosaics of every colour, including gold. They had their workshops somewhere among the ruins of the Campus Martius where for several generations they carried on their trade. Surrounded on every side by classical columns and entablatures of precious marbles their material was almost limitless. They ruthlessly levelled to the ground and sawed these remains into roundels, squares, rectangles and scrolls of all sizes and shapes or cut them into fragmentary chips. The Cosmati school also numbered scupltors and even architects. Examples of their sculpture are found in several tomb effigies, and of their architecture, in the beautiful cloisters of San Giovanni in Laterano and San Paolo fuori le Mura, which they signed with their names. Assiduously they studied and copied antique models, at the same time developing a vigorous and pronounced style of their own. The art of the Cosmati reached its highest perfection between the ends of the twelfth and thirteenth centuries. Their renown spread throughout Christendom and Abbot Richard Ware of Westminster succeeded in inducing one of them, by name Petrus Oderisi,[6] to travel from Rome with him all the way to England, bringing slabs of the highly prized red and green imperial porphyry. Petrus applied them to the shrine of Edward the Confessor and the wonderfully exotic tomb of Henry III in Westminster Abbey. When it came to laying the sanctuary pavement in front of the high altar the supply of porphyry ran out and because of the high cost of transport no more was sent. Instead Petrus did the best he could with inferior English substitutes including grey Purbeck marble and coloured glass which he cut into chips of the requisite shapes.

[6] Petrus Oderisi, or his son, made Clement IV's gorgeous tomb at Viterbo with Gothic trefoil canopy and recumbent effigy.

Members of the Cosmati school did not confine their work at Santa Maria in Cosmedin to the floor of the nave and aisles. Less than half way up the nave, and raised by one step over the crypt, is that rare and compelling feature of a Roman mediaeval church, the choir, or *schola cantorum*. Low marble walls carefully restored in 1898, divide but do not separate the schola from the body of the church. The panels of the walls are of Brescia and Carara marbles and the floor of the schola is paved in *opus alexandrinum*. Against the north and south walls rise Cardinal Alfanus's pair of pulpits, or *ambons*, one for the gospel, which was chanted by a deacon facing the sanctuary, and the other for the epistle, chanted facing across the church. They are the most perfect of their kind in existence. The word is derived from the Greek, αμβων meaning "I walk up," and is explained by the construction of steps leading to a reading desk at the top of each, and in the case of the epistle desk descending the other side. Compared with those later ambons in Santa Maria in Ara Coeli the design is extremely straightforward and shows that the Cosmati were capable of the highest sculptural effects when they reduced their decorative inlay to a minimum. Here for example the style is rather Romanesque than Byzantine. The ball-capped posts and the pilasters of the epistle desk are carved in a parchment pattern of simple, clean moulds and the acanthus border which frames the whole composition is a model of restrained and forceful decoration. The three upright panels of the desk are of a claret porphyry and the horizontal panel below is of Brescia marble. A corresponding panel on the back of the epistle ambon, facing the south aisle, is of grey porphyry, an exceedingly rare material. The steps on the east side of the epistle ambon are flanked by a twisted column encrusted with glittering mosaic and glass[7] and crowned by a composite capital. The column is upheld by the paws of a couchant lion, of a proud yet docile mien, carved in oriental alabaster.

[7] The presence of glass tesserae is evidence of late, decadent Cosmatesque work, when the rarer materials were exhausted.

This is the paschal candlestick and an inscription records that it was presented at the end of the thirteenth century by a Dominican friar, oddly enough called Pasqualis, and described as "*vir probus et doctus.*" The use of paschal candlesticks dates from the first Christian centuries. Their origin was of course Jewish and probably derived from the famous seven-branched candlestick which Titus brought in triumph to Rome after the capture of Jerusalem in A.D. 70. The early Christian candelabra were made of metal, but all of them have long ago been melted down. They were traditionally set beside the epistle ambon and bore a wax candle which was lit on Holy Saturday and extinguished on Ascension Day.

The *schola* is separated from the sanctuary by a marble screen called the *iconostasis* (literally, the image bearer) which is extended right across both aisles. Its counterpart in English churches is the chancel screen which separates the congregation from the choir as well as from the sanctuary. Here, however, the origin of the iconostasis was, as its name implies, Greek and not Latin, and its object to conceal from both choir and congregation the elevation of the Host and thus invest the Sacrament with an awful mystery. In Greek Orthodox churches such screens habitually reach the springing of the vault in several tiers and so render the sanctuary absolutely invisible. In this case curtains between the columns were deemed adequate and during the solemn parts of the Mass were discreetly drawn across. The existing iconostasis is a faithful reconstruction of what Alfanus erected in the twelfth century as the modern Latin inscription upon it informs us. The moulds and acanthus patterns reproduced are the same as those upon the ambons and the Chancellor's monument in the portico. The columns rest upon bases connected by dwarf walls, containing on their west faces horizontal panels of Cosmatesque work. On the east faces four panels of Pope Adrian's time, discarded in the twelfth century, have been reinserted. They display carvings in flat relief of interlaced knots, lilies and flower heads. One panel includes a cross, adorned with a motif of twisted threads on the arms of which perching peacocks, symbols of the Resurrection, drink from two-handled beakers. The character of these eighth-century carvings is essentially Byzantine. Unfortunately they are today totally obscured by a pair of ignoble wooden pew stalls, which can, however, be shifted without much difficulty.

The *schola cantorum* formed part of the mediaeval liturgical scheme, rigorous and disciplined, which the renaissance prelates, actuated by latitudinarian notions, particularly resented. They consequently took steps to sweep away these obnoxious constructions in great numbers. In Rome only one other specimen, and that of a still earlier date, is preserved—at San Clemente. It too is a reconstruction and was brought to its present position from the lower church during the excavations of a hundred years ago.

On the far side of the iconostasis, upon another raised pavement looms the high altar under its great canopy. The canopy is one of the rare gothic architectural features to be found in Rome and is the work of Cosma Deodatus—"Deodatus me fecit" is incised upon the entablature. It was erected in the late thirteenth century, clearly under the influence of the Florentine Arnolfus di Cambio. Four columns of red Egyptian granite support the white hood, its trefoil front and prickly finials encrusted with mosaics. It shelters a Roman bath of red granite, given legs by Adrian and by Alfanus a slab top which is dated 1123, to serve as altar. Within this altar reposes the skull of Saint Valentine, the beloved of lovers the world over, which on every 14th February is brought out, crowned with roses and venerated. The canopy was so extravagantly admired and imitated by Church of England architects of the 1870's—the uninspired altar canopy in alabaster and mosaic at Peterborough Cathedral and Gilbert Scott's magnified replica in the Albert Memorial instantly come to mind—that I find difficulty in judging it objectively as genuine medieval work. Far more satisfactory to my taste are the canopies at San

Lorenzo Fuori and San Giorgio in Velabro with their tiered hoods, like wedding cakes, on slender colonettes, both fashioned by the Cosmati but in the Romanesque and not Gothic style, and so ignored by fashionable Victorian copyists under the contentious influence of Ruskin.

Behind the canopy and raised by yet another step is the presbytery. Its floor of *opus sectile*—which merely means thin slices of coloured marbles cut into geometrical shapes forming patterns like those of an Ispahan carpet—is of Pope Adrian's time. Built into the central apse is the bishop's marble chair over a slab of porphyry. In accordance with a tradition inherited from the pagan tribune where the judge presided in the middle of a half circle of lawyers, the bishop's chair is set above the presbyters' bench, which follows the curve of the apse. It is a simplified version of Vasaletus's ambitious throne in the Duomo at Anagni. A terminal lion with chubby feet supports the end of each arm. The seat is much worn. From the back rises like a halo a disk inlaid with Cosmatesque mosaic and bearing on the rim the words *Alfanus fieri tibi fecit Virgo Maria.*

Yes, on the whole, the twelfth century Chancellor Alfanus must receive credit for the greater part of the adornment that survives in Santa Maria in Cosmedin. Surely, too, no small measure of praise is due to his late nineteenth-century successor, Cardinal Deacon de Ruggiero, who brought about the restoration of this unique mediaeval church to its present exemplary condition.

BIBLIOGRAPHY

Guidebook entitled *Chiesa di Santa Maria in Cosmedin, Cenno Storico*, 1950.

EDWARD HUTTON. *The Cosmati*, 1950.

C. A. HEMANS. *Historic and Monumental Rome*, 1874.

M. ARMELLINI. *Le Chiese di Roma*, 1891.

C. A. CUMMINGS. *A History of Architecture in Italy*, 1901

A. L. FROTHINGHAM. *Monuments of Christian Rome*, 1908.

RENAISSANCE I

――――◦◦◉◦◦――――

Il Tempietto

NOT for nothing has Rome acquired that rather trite title—the Eternal City. There are other capitals, notably in the Middle East, with foundations older by several millenia. Such are Ur, Nineveh and Thebes. There are even in Europe Knossos of Crete and Tiryns in the Greek Peloponnese, which flourished in the distant civilizations called Aegean. But their histories, once pullulant with glorious events, have long ago been buried in the dust. The history of Rome on the contrary has been continuous for over two thousand seven hundred years, and is today not yet over. In spite of terrible eras, when barbarians from the north overwhelmed her ancient civilization, when her own children, reduced to the extremes of despair consumed as fast as the foreign hordes her own past, when the arts were reduced to the lowest ebb, and Rome must have seemed to the eye of a dispassionate observer moribund indeed—then slowly, miraculously she recovered. She recovered from the appalling insult delivered by the first Christian Emperor in depriving her of the seat of the ancient world: from the incursions of Goths, Vandals, Lombards and Franks: from the sacks of Alaric, Genseric, Guiscard and the Constable of Bourbon: from the enslavement of Normans, Austrians and Nazis: from the fanatical creeds of paganism, Catholicism and Fascism: from the iconoclasm of her own popes, princes and people: from pestilences, earthquakes and inundations. She has outlived all these disasters and is still alive.

The secret of Rome's survival up to date has been abundantly clear. It is quite simply a faithful adherence to her classical tradition. Once that tradition is abandoned,

Rome is finished. Had she lost sight of it in the Middle Ages and adopted the Gothic style, she would have forfeited continuity with her great architectural past which she might never have recaptured. Had she built half a dozen churches in the style of Santa Maria sopra Minerva she would have been finished, just as Venice will be finished if she builds as many palaces on the Grand Canal in the style of Burton the Fifty Shilling Tailor. The merits of the Gothic style (certainly the most sublime the world has yet evolved) and that of Mr. Frank Lloyd Wright are entirely beside the point. It is of no ultimate consequence, as we have seen, that mediaeval Romans from the Pope downwards systematically treated ancient monuments as quarries, whence they extracted columns and entablatures because they were too dis-organized and impoverished of ideas to build with new materials to new designs. Roman architecture was eventually saved by this negative iconoclasm, for gradually the spirit released out of the palaces and temples of the Emperors by the assiduous marble cutters and lime burners in the fora took refuge in the minds of these men and propagated a new offspring. The Cosmatesque art arose, phoenix-like out of the midst of the quarries and furnaces. Once again in history victorious Philistines were made to bow the knee before the ghosts of past creators. The task of eradicating a deeply entrenched culture proved hopeless before their limited inspirations. At first they had nothing better to substitute. People cannot go on hacking and burning for ever unless they are actuated by more than a vague urge to keep alive. Just as the early Romans first saw virtue in the ruins of the Etruscan civilization which they had brought low, so the Cosmati suddenly realized that these old bits of marble were not so contemptible after all. More intelligent than the barbarians of our own century they grew to admire what they were destroying, and attempted to reproduce the ancient patterns in their own works. They were not so vain and stupid as to fear that by emulating a proved and developed style they thereby ran the risk of lacking originality (as if more than a handful of the greatest artists in the world's history have been original) and merely reproducing works sterile and without character. As it happened, the sculpture of the Cosmati was far from mere copying. It soon became imbued with an intense spiritual fervour fully reflective of the age of deepest Christian devotion. The Cosmati were the initiators of a Roman proto-Renaissance which has never been adequately appreciated. The twelfth and thirteenth centuries made the Roman arts very much alive again. The City had been saved. The dawn of a revived humanism was on the horizon, and in its train the greatest rebirth of the arts known to man. Paganism after all was not dead.

The architectural Renaissance, as everyone knows, was not first experienced in Rome. The mysterious growth had been budding in Tuscany and Lombardy for a hundred years already. When it spread to Rome it was in full bloom. It was manifested there by an individual also in his full maturity. When Donato d'Agnolo, commonly known as Bramante Lazzari, arrived at the papal court to seek employment, he was a man well in his fifties. For a quarter of a century he had been practising architecture in Milan and the surrounding duchy. There his style, although very individual, was distinguished by the integration of tight, jewel-like surface-units common to all the great Lombardy architects of the quattrocento, including da Maiano and Michelozzo. The moment Bramante reached Rome he plunged into a deep study of ancient monuments with the result that his style changed forthwith. It became free from sculptural ornament. The minute goldsmith panels of his earlier years were abandoned. Instead Bramante adopted the spatial, constructional forms of the ancients. He did not live to build a great deal in Rome, but what he built was in the developed High Renaissance style and, as such, marked perhaps the greatest architectural advance in the City since the first classical monuments had arisen in the time of the Republic. Nothing so startling in style was to be seen in Rome again until the 1920's when the first modernistic blocks arose in Parioli and the new suburbs.

Rather conveniently and quite truthfully we can say that the architectural Renaissance showed its first signs in Rome in 1500, in which year Bramante began the little cloisters adjoining the church of Santa Maria della Pace. They are a composition of marvellous simplicity and grace, something strikingly, undeniably classical, yet from the word "go" breaking the rules of the orders in a characteristically Bramantesque *gusto grande* by having columns in the top walk set over the arch-keys of the lower. This particular touch of unorthodoxy recalls that other when Bramante strangely inserted single columns in the middle of his windows in the apse of Santa Maria della Grazie in Milan. At once, in a flash as it were, the Roman Renaissance asserts its independence of rules, its latitude and its individuality, while at the same time confining its idiosyncrasies within the strictest limitations. The structure of classical architecture is analogous to that of the sonnet. The rules of the orders are strictly laid down, and their spirit rather than letter, regarded as sacrosanct. Whosoever transgresses them does so at his peril. The man of genius may dare and the results may be praiseworthy. The man of mediocre talent does well to abide by them or he will go seriously wrong. Yet in spite of the limitations set by the rules of classical building and the sonnet, the greatest variety of beauties in both may be achieved, whether the architects and poets rigidly conform like Palladio and Milton, or take liberties like Michelangelo and Gerard Manley Hopkins.

The Renaissance in effect imposed no straightjacket upon the architect's invention, as you have only to see for yourself in one morning's casual walk round Rome. What, to take three examples of renaissance palaces within a random circuit of the city, could be more different in everything but style than Bramante's Giraud (or Torlonia), Antonio Sangallo's Farnese and Raphael's Vidoni, all three built within a decade? All are composed of three stages of horizontal rows of windows. Yet they differ from one another as do chalk, cheese and cucumber. Or if you prefer more poetical analogies, the first is a lyric, the second an ode and the third an epic. One is spontaneous, one measured, one heroic. You may describe them as you feel inclined, so long as you are agreed that all three are poems of high degree and in classical metre. It is doubtful whether ancient Roman architecture ever allowed such freedom of invention. It was far too rigid and coercive, as Vitruvius would have us to understand. But although Vitruvius's gospel was unearthed and repromulgated to attentive but suspicious Italian ears in the fifteenth century and although Serlio, Vignola and Palladio in the following century reiterated it with most solemn warnings against transgressors, their fulminations were ultimately in vain. The Romans of the Renaissance, like those of today, were not made of the same tractable stuff as the ancients. They would not (and will not, as Mussolini was to discover) submit to dictation, only to guidance. An architect like Michelangelo could not be kept on Vitruvius's bearing rein any more than Borromini could be curbed by official disapproval in the seventeenth century. The mainspring of their independence was of course the humanistic philosophy on which they had been nurtured, and whence the renaissance arts sprang. This philosophy implied the reversal of the outworn mediaeval theory of corporate obedience, and a release of individual self-expression. And individualism is the hall mark of the Renaissance. The architecture of the middle ages was regimented and anonymous, notwithstanding its apparent slapdash methods of design and construction and its indulgence of the whims of the sculptural mason; the architecture of the Renaissance was by comparison unrestrained and free in spite of the rules of the Five Orders and the almost mechanical use of conventional ornament.

In 1502 Bramante was commissioned to design and erect on the Janiculum hill at the expense of King Ferdinand and Queen Isabella of Aragon and Castile a monument of great religious implication. This was the little temple, or *Tempietto*, in the cloister adjacent to the north side of the church of San Pietro in Montorio. The church and its attendant monastery had been entrusted by Sixtus IV in the fifteenth century to the Minor Observants, the stricter branch of the Franciscan Order who live in small communities entirely on charity and own no landed property. The church was at the time of the gift in a deplorably ruinous condition and the Minor Observants importuned the King and Queen of Spain, who were known to favour their order, to rebuild it for them. Ferdinand and Isabella promised to do so on the condition that the brothers through their prayers obtained for them the birth of a son. Fortunately the prayers of the Minor Observants bore fruit—which scarcely ripened[1]—and the royal couple gratefully fulfilled their promise. Towards the end of the century the church was entirely rebuilt, possibly by Baccio Pontelli, at their expense.

The site of San Pietro was highly sacred to the Christians of mediaeval Rome. There had always been a church there since Constantine founded an oratory in the fourth century. The early fathers held that the very site was Ararat—and not the Armenian mountain of that name—whereon Noah's ark rested when the flood waters receded and the progenitor of a new race of mankind first set foot on disembarking. This legend was important enough but it was linked to another of even greater significance. The rock on which the ship of salvation was stranded was the very same rock on which the Church of the world was founded. Here by divine coincidence Saint Peter on the 29th June, A.D. 67 was crucified head downwards at his own request because he was not worthy to meet the same fate as his Lord, and as a sinner it behoved him to face the dust whence he came and to which he must return. By the eighth century the legend was universally accepted and notwithstanding that it was

---

[1] In the centre of the transept of Santo Tomás at Avila lies the exquisite effigy of the young Prince Juan, the only son of Ferdinand and Isabella. He died aged 18.

later disproved, is still vehemently maintained by the bare-footed brown Brother who seems to be permanently on duty at the call of visitors. But, alas, the tradition was based upon a misinterpretation by the mediaeval historians of one Latin word. The Apocryphal Acts disclose that Saint Peter was crucified on the *spina*, or middle line, *inter duas metas*, the scene of many subsequent Christian martyrdoms. In the eighth century the word *meta* had lost its original meaning and was applied to tombs of pyramidal shape, of which two only survived, those of Caius Cestius and of Romulus (the last subsequently destroyed). By a muddled process of scientific measurement and wishful inference so dear to the mediaeval mind the location of the *spina* was exactly fixed on the central axis of what is now Bramante's Tempietto. In the middle of the sixteenth century the precise Latin meaning of *meta*—namely a goal—came to be properly translated and accordingly the spot on which the Apostle's crucifix had been planted was shown to have been between the two goals of Nero's Circus, now marked by the great obelisk in the *piazza* of Saint Peter. At the same time Pope Paul III, as though to show his contempt for this incon-venient revelation, decreed that whenever a priest said Mass in the Tempietto at least one soul was to be freed from Purgatory. Certainly the brown Brother of the Minor Observants is blissfully undeterred by the disclosure of four centuries ago which modern archaeologists have confirmed. In showing you into the crypt of the Tempietto he will scoop up from the middle of the floor, where the base of the crucifix was supposed to have been set a handful of the fine golden sand from which the hill, *mons aureus*, takes its name. The brown Brother will reverently explain to you through gusts of garlic how the common dust was changed into this golden sand beneath the dying gaze of the Prince of the Apostles.

The "Catholic" King and his Queen naturally reposed implicit faith in the legends both of Ararat and Saint Peter's martyrdom. The exact area, marked by the miraculous trickle of golden sand was holy ground crying aloud for some permanent memorial to enshrine it. What architect could be more worthy than the Pope's new protégé recently arrived from Lombardy with a reputation for having built churches in the latest style of architecture? Ferdinand and Isabella were of the most uncompromising orthodoxy in religious matters, but like all royal and noble patrons of renaissance times in the forefront of fashion as regards the arts. The sponsors of Christopher Columbus were not afraid of risking a small architectural venture.

Small the Tempietto undoubtedly is, but as a work of art and as an archetype it is of immense stature, of far-reaching influence. Size, I need hardly say, is absolutely no criterion in assessing the merits of architecture. Scale on the other hand is everything. Helvellyn in relation to the neighbouring peaks of the miniature Cumbrian range is every bit as majestic and awe-inspiring as Monte Rosa surrounded by its fellow Alpine giants. So too every part of the Tempietto is perfectly related to the whole structure. It has all the dignity and solemnity of Saint Peter's and is far more beautiful. It is as beautiful in its economy of line and form as any building of the ancient Romans known to us. Even Palladio acknowledged this claim and the measure of his praise lies in the fact that he felt justified in illustrating the Tempietto, the only building of modern times, in the fourth book of his *Quattro Libri*, which was otherwise devoted to the masterpieces of the ancients. The pious disciple of Vitruvius classed it with the superlative temples of the world he knew, with the Pantheon, Santa Costanza, the Baptistery of Constantine at the Lateran, the Temple of Vesta at Tivoli: even with the Temple of Castor and Pollux, and, outside Rome, with the Temples at Pola and Nîmes. In his opinion it reached the apex of building during the High Renaissance. Architecture could hardly go further than this. After the grandeur of imperial Rome, wrote Palladio, architecture like all the other sciences and arts declined into barbaric darkness, until not a trace of fine proportion or style in building [*ornata maniera di fabricare*] was remembered. "But then in the time of our fathers and grandfathers," he went on, "architecture re-emerged from the darkness in which it had so long remained. Once more it began to reveal itself [*cominciò a lasciarsi rivedere nella luce del mondo*] for under the pontificate of Julius II Bramante that most excellent man and student of the monuments of the ancients, himself raised the most beautiful buildings in Rome. . . ." It is interesting to note that Palladio considered Bramante the first to reintroduce correct and beautiful architecture [*il primo a metter in luce la buona e bella Architettura*]. The great pioneer from Milan was followed by Michelangelo, Sansovino, Peruzzi, Antonio Sangallo, Sanmichele, Vignola and others. But Bramante's illustrious predecessors of the quattrocento, Brunelleschi, Alberti, Michelozzo and da Maiano are not referred to. In other words Palladio classed them among the barbarians fumbling in the darkness. In his eyes the golden days of the Florentine architectural Renaissance counted for nothing. His reasons are not far to seek. The fifteenth-century masters were improperly grounded in the rules of the Orders. They were unversed in Vitruvius. Palladio necessarily attributed the triumph of Bramante to his undeviating adherence to the tenets of that ancient legislator. In a sense of course he was right. Bramante was known to have measured all the great monuments that remained in Rome. He was steeped in Vitruvian lore, and his Tempietto was a classical revival. Was it therefore merely a dumb reproduction of the antique? And did it express no more than the beauty of an echo? And was life scarcely stirring there?[2]

Because of his great learning and genius Bramante was equipped to improve upon the ancients. Vasari in his life of the architect conceded as much when he wrote without hyperbole: "for if the Greeks invented that architecture which the Romans imitated, Bramante did more than the latter, since he not only imitated, but, imparting to us what

[2] Geoffrey Scott—*The Architecture of Humanism.*

they had taught, in a new and ameliorated form, he added unwonted graces and beauties to the art, which we receive enobled and embellished by his efforts." There were several examples of circular temples in and around Rome in which he could find precedents and from which he must have borrowed ideas for his essay at San Pietro in Montorio. But in no respects was his Tempietto a slavish copy of any one of them. There were the Temples of Vesta in the Forum Romanum, of Mater Matuta and of the Invincible Hercules, both in the Forum Boarium, and of Vesta again at Tivoli. The first which had been discovered in 1489 was in an excellent state of preservation when Bramante saw it;[3] but although its foundations were the oldest it had frequently been rebuilt in Roman times and lastly in a style which Vitruvius condemned as debased. The second was more or less in the same condition as today, thus being a fairly complete example of Augustan architecture apart from the dome which was, and is, missing. The third was then very ruinous and has now completely disappeared. The fourth which was intact (apart from the dome) was considered by renaissance architects a specimen of the purest and best Roman style (it was illustrated by Serlio and Palladio) since it dated from the end of the Republic. The Temples of Mater Matuta and of Vesta at Tivoli (which incidentally greatly resembled one another) were therefore the archetypes which Bramante probably aspired to emulate. Moreover we have Vasari's word that he spent more time studying remains at Tivoli than anywhere else in or around Rome.

To start with, Bramante's intentions at San Pietro were far more ambitious than his executed work leads us to suppose. Vasari praises unstintedly the beauties of the Tempietto. "Nothing," he says, "more perfectly conceived, more graceful, or more beautiful can be imagined whether as regards arrangement, proportion or variety," and then adds, "how much more beautiful it would have been if the whole of the cloister had been finished according to the plan

[3] It was levelled to the ground in 1549. A fragment of it was restored in 1930.

which may be seen." The plan may still be seen in the Uffizi Galleries. It is of a circle within a circle. Bramante then meant the Tempietto to stand within a circular colonnade, having four entrances between four spade-shaped lesser chapels and eight niches—to be the hub whence radiated a catherine wheel shooting off a rhythm of symmetrical sparks. As it stands, the Tempietto is far too cramped within the present square courtyard, which was made to look more confined when the lower arcades of three cloister walks were filled sometime during the nineteenth century. In consequence the sun of a winter morning barely penetrates below the finial and the cross of the dome. In full summer it only reaches the whole Tempietto when high in the heavens and then plunges the cornices into uncompromising shadow.

The plan of the Tempietto itself shows great ingenuity. Completely circular outside, inside by a dexterous arrangement of four deep niches it has become a Greek cross. The deep niches have shell heads and are separated by Doric pilasters.[4] The exterior of the body is divided into alternate shallow niches with shell heads, and square recesses. There are four doorways besides. The body is surrounded by a peristyle of sixteen Doric columns of grey granite, their capitals and bases being of marble. The columns are made to diminish at the tops and bottoms and swell to their fullest diameter at the lowest third of their height. The four ancient circular temples to which I have referred had peristyles of eighteen to twenty-one columns, whereas only that of the Invincible Hercules was of the Doric order, the other three being of the Corinthian order. Bramante's reduction of the number of columns so as to leave intervals for niches and windows and his choice of the Doric order imply that he aimed at robustness rather than elegance. His peristyle is moreover set on a very squat platform,

---

[4] The crypt was entirely redecorated in 1628. It is approached by a stair formed within a segment of the three steps on which the temple is set. By means of this ingenious device the circle of the stylobate remains unbroken.

raised on three steps which descend evenly into the pavement. In this respect he followed the Temple of Mater Matuta, for the columns of the other three ancient temples were raised on deep platforms.

The frieze of the peristyle is carved with much vigour and delicacy. Between the triglyphs (and you will notice how every third falls accurately above the centre of each column) the architect introduced emblems in flattish relief pertaining to Saint Peter—namely a chalice, lamp, cross, open book, mitre, cross keys, etcetera—in place of the conventional ram's head and circle. The entablature (lacking the emblems however) is repeated within the peristyle. The ceiling of the peristyle Bramante made flat and decorated with two rows of coffers, each with a central rosette of different pattern (except over the principal entrance where there is only one coffer with a single large rose). Here he was evidently mindful of the Temple of Vesta at Tivoli. The peristyle is finished with a feature entirely unknown to the ancients, which gives it a crowning beauty, namely the continuous range of wasp-waisted balusters. Of these every fourth carefully falls into place above a column. Bernini was so enamoured of this combination of peristyle and balustrade and the sense of movement it engendered, that he followed it with scarcely any deviation in an unexecuted design to clothe the northern apse of Santa Maria Maggiore.

Bramante's need of a balustrade was of course the consequence of his major innovation, the drum and dome. The grace and loveliness of his dome surpass all the tributes that four and a half centuries have lavished upon them. The dome was a step towards his greater essay at Saint Peter's Cathedral, which never got further than paper. It was by no means the first to be built in renaissance Italy, for there was Brunelleschi's octagonal masterpiece at Florence. But it was the first to be designed in spherical shape. The temples of the ancient Romans had been covered with low saucer domes not raised on drums but slightly stepped above cornice level (that of the Pantheon is the only surviving example), so the problem of how to crown the entablature of their peristyles never confronted them. Bramante treated the drum as he did the body of the temple by contriving bays of windows blocked and unblocked and shell-headed niches alternately. Palladio in his woodcut filled the niches with standing figures which probably never existed. The niches were doubtless designed as much for pictorial effect of light and shade as for the function of lightening the load of the dome. Bramante's *coup de grâce* was the royal arms of Aragon and Castille on the snow white finial.

Serlio remarked that "this temple sheweth too high for the breadth." He was obviously judging it from an elevational drawing. Indeed I suspect that if it stood in the open, free from the surrounding court buildings, then the upper stage which is much emphasized by the wide band between drum and dome, might appear disproportionately high. But Bramante never intended the Tempietto to stand in the open and be seen from a distance. On the contrary he expressly designed it to be enclosed, not, as I have pointed out, by the present rectangular court, but a circular colonnade. In realizing that it would only be seen from close quarters he exactly calculated what allowance of additional height to give it. A more serious criticism is that the niches, windows and doors of the body are too crammed against the pilasters. The marble head of the principal door even cuts right across the flanking pilasters. This fault, for which Bramante had a precedent in the Pantheon attic, did not escape Inigo Jones's notice. He jotted down in the margin of his volume of Palladio's *Quattro Libri:* "Temple of Bramante. This tempietto I observed often being in Rome, *anno* 1614. And if Bramante had made no *contro colloni* pr pilasters in the wall of the cella but only quadratur [*sic*] he might then I say have made the door bigger and not have broken the order of pilasters," whose presence Jones only deemed permissible upon the body of a large temple. I daresay he was right in wishing the pilasters were not there, so as to leave the surrounds of the openings (if that is what he meant by *quadratur*) free upon the plain circumference. Of the four ancient circular temples only that of Vesta in the Forum had engaged columns upon its body and the arrangement probably influenced Bramante in designing the Tempietto. But I do not agree with Jones in thinking the doorway thereby required widening. In itself the doorway is admirably proportioned to the building. It is certainly a fact that the niches and windows of the drum are far better related to their intervening panels than are those of the body to the pilasters.

Notwithstanding this one imperfection, which was at any rate deliberate, the Tempietto reaches the consummate peak of High Renaissance architecture. To the uninitiated this small, unassuming structure in faded ochre wash, bearing the recent scars and graffiti which are the ubiquitous hall marks of the tourist industry, may at first appear a slight disappointment. Why, you may ask, so much extravagant fuss about this rather pretty toy hidden away in too confined a court? It is not enough for me to answer that if you do not see the point of the Tempietto during your first visit then you surely will after your sixth. There are presumably a number of valid reasons for the fuss. To begin with, howsoever you or I may judge it, the Tempietto was considered by Bramante's contemporaries and successors to be an architectural triumph of the first magnitude. It made him at once famous all over Italy. Sixteenth-century artists amongst the greatest in history, like Michelangelo and Palladio, flocked to see it, measure it, draw it, discuss it and write about it. With what you may think their exaggerated reverence for antiquity these men pronounced that it vied with, no, even excelled the architecture of the ancients. Seventeenth-century artists still remained spellbound by it. Bernini reproduced it in miniature as a tabernacle in bronze enriched with goldsmith's work of lapis-lazuli for the Chapel of the Holy Sacrament in Saint Peter's. Wren reproduced it in his first design for the west towers of Saint Paul's Cathedral, and Soufflot for the drum and dome of the

Pantheon in Paris. In the eighteenth century it kept reappearing in modified forms upon garden temples in French and English country gentlemen's parks like Ledoux's Rotonde de Monçeaux, Hawksmoor's Mausoleum at Castle Howard, Kent's Temple of Virtue at Stowe, Gibbs's Temple at Hackwood, and Adam's Temple of Victory at Audley End. In the nineteenth century it was still being reproduced. You may see a gilt model of it serving as the tabernacle of Saint Francis Xavier's Catholic Church in Hereford, which dates from William IV's reign.

It is not perhaps a sufficient answer that the Tempietto marks the first definite link-up of the architecture of the moderns with that of the ancients, or the final break with that of the middle ages. In this small structure Bramante utterly discarded minute surface detail, the use of which the quattrocento architects of Tuscany and Lombardy still retained from the mediaeval builders. Instead he relied upon the simpler ancient elements of line and mass to fulfil his decorative needs. These elements cry out and cannot be overlooked. They consist in the horizontal curves of the steps, balustrade and cornice of the drum, in the vertical lines of the columns of the peristyle, which without interruption are carried through the balusters, the panels of the drum and the ribs of the dome up into the cross. The skilful manner in which these lines are interrelated gives the Tempietto an almost cosmic quality. Bramante was a master of perspective, as you may judge from his frescoes and engravings of architectural fantasies at Bergamo and Milan and from his astonishing stucco apse of San Satiro in the last city. He was also highly versed in geometry, as you may perceive from his Scala a Chiocciola in the Vatican—the archetype of those spiral staircases by Vignola, Bernini and the builder of Chambord—an accomplishment recognized by Raphael who in the School of Athens depicted him as a venerable baldhead bending over a pair of compasses and a slate in the rôle of Archimedes. In these respects he fulfilled the exclusive prerequisites of a renaissance architect laid down by Alberti, namely skill in the subsidiary arts of painting and mathematics—*nelle altre non curo che sia dotto*. As it happened, he delighted also in poetry and music, for he wrote verse, how well we do not know, and, Vasari tells us, performed tolerably on the lyre. These then were additional accomplishments of this versatile genius who was entirely without jealousy or rancour.

In the Tempietto Bramante had through the conjunction of intellect and skill achieved the purest and most lucid architectonic expression of which man is capable. He had struck a magic chord and succeeded in creating something inexplicably and indefinably great, an aesthetic abstract, a work of art. I do not suppose that a building which answers to this description needs any further justification.

BIBLIOGRAPHY

A. PALLADIO. Fourth Book of *Architettura*, 1570.

S. SERLIO. *Regole Generali de Architectura*, Vol. 3, 1540.

INIGO JONES. Marginal Notes in his copy of Palladio's *Quattro Libri dell 'Architettura*.

G. VASARI. The Architect Bramante, from *The Lives of the Painters*, etc.

P. M. LETAROUILLY. *Edifices de Rome Moderne*, 1840–57.

EMILIO LAVAGNINO. *Guidebook*.

M. ARMELLINI. *Le Chiese di Roma*, 1891.

COSTANTINO BARONI. *Bramante*, c. 1945.

RENAISSANCE II

------⊃∘◉∘⊂------

Palazzo Pietro Massimo Alle Colonne

I HAVE delayed so long in referring to domestic and have up till now dealt so exclusively with temple architecture that you may well have decided that my interests rejected the first category. This is not so. The fact is that in palace architecture the metropolis of the world lagged behind the cities of Tuscany and the north Italian states during the middle ages. Whereas Florence, Bologna and Padua, for examples, are distinguished by their pre-renaissance palaces, whose massive forbidding walls and exiguous gothic windows frown at each other across the narrow streets, no palace of the mediaeval Romans has survived intact. In the late middle ages noble families were still dwelling in converted fortresses like the Casa dei Crescenzi, or in rude defensive towers, like the Torre delle Milizie. Even in the fifteenth century palace architecture was extremely rare. The small Palazzo Capranica and the large Palazzo di Venezia, both dating from the 1450's, are about the only two exceptions. The first with its quadrangular tower is still basically a fortress with some applied renaissance features in windows and doorcases. The second, which is of a style more transitional (it is a major work of quattrocento architecture) stands in a class of its own and has no fellow in Rome. Until the advent of Bramante with the High Renaissance Rome was not a city of palaces. Thenceforward the face of the city became entirely altered, for the sixteenth and seventeenth centuries gave to its streets the opulent and patrician character which has endured until our own time.

Bramante and his disciples were the instruments which brought about the change from church to palace building in Rome. It is of course true that during the Renaissance new churches not infrequently replaced what stood before. For instance, Bramante himself was the first architect to be entrusted by the papacy with the rebuilding of Saint Peter's. Under his direction Constantine's basilica was demolished to make way for the gigantic renaissance cathedral that exists today. For three hundred years the process of recasing Romanesque churches in a classical guise or entirely re-edifying them on old sites continued. Only rarely, however, were new churches built on new sites. Palaces, on the contrary, were innovations. They supplied a new social and economic need and arose out of the ruins of ancient monuments or upon the sites of mediaeval hovels. The first of the palaces to appear on a scale of domestic magnificence hitherto unknown to Rome was that of the Cancelleria. It sprang, a monstrous phoenix, out of the foundations of Pompey's Theatre before the close of the fifteenth century but was not completed until the second decade of the sixteenth. Although the Palazzo Cancelleria was begun before Bramante reached Rome, its style is so reflective of his known work in Rome, notably the Palazzo Giraud built in 1506, that it must unquestionably owe its ultimate form to his influence.[1]

Bramante's palace architecture which was largely derived from the Tuscan quattrocento and in particular from Alberti's famous façade of the Palazzo Ruccelai in Florence consisted of immensely strong, almost impregnable lower storeys, of which the only reluctant alleviations were small prison-like windows with grills and an entrance porch in the Doric order: and of two independent upper storeys each striped with flat pilasters cutting through the overall horizontal rustication. It is obvious that Bramante could not altogether dissociate his conception of a renaissance palace from the mediaeval needs of defence against outside assault.

---

[1] Vasari wrote that Bramante "was invited to take part with other eminent architects in the greater number of the consultations which were held respecting the Palace of San Giorgio [Cancelleria] and the Church of San Lorenzo in Damaso [a part of it]," but that "the works of this fabric were conducted by Antonio Monticavallo."

As a result his palaces remained self-protective, robust and essentially masculine.

By contrast the architecture of Bramante's immediate follower, only subordinate to him in the hierarchy of Roman architects of the High Renaissance, namely Baldassare Peruzzi, was more feminine. Peruzzi's architecture was perhaps only an advance upon his predecessor's in the sense that the elegant Ionic order is an advance upon the homely Doric, because it came after. The consequent architecture of Peruzzi was undeniably more refined and even more delicate than Bramante's. Peruzzi was, we are told by Vasari, a man of almost excessive sensibility—which in the eyes of unsympathetic observers verged sometimes on silliness—and supreme tranquillity of mind. The biographer speaks, not without a touch of disdain, of his "heavenly endowments." Is it therefore surprising that his architecture is singularly unaffected and tender? A less compulsive artist than the older man, he accordingly makes a less popular, and more esoteric appeal. He is above all the artist's artist.

Peruzzi is first heard of working in Rome in 1503 under Bramante upon designs for the new Saint Peter's. He was at that time a young man of twenty-two, immensely learned, immensely versatile, already amply fulfilling the Renaissance's conception of an architect in his mastery of more than the requisite number of subsidiary arts. In addition to his skill as a painter and mathematician, he was an astrologer and inventor of movable scenery. In his childhood he is said to have haunted the workshops of the goldsmiths. Before he was twenty years old he had left his home in the neighbourhood of Volterra and became the pupil of Pinturicchio while the great painter was composing frescoes for Cardinal Francesco Piccolomini in the cathedral library at Siena. Was it perhaps at Siena that Peruzzi acquired his first sense of that "architectonic decoration," which in the vaulted arcades and pilaster panels encrusted like jewellery with candelabrum and dolphin ornament is the only positive

virtue allowed by Mr. Berenson to the sensitive and gentle
Pinturicchio?

We know that the very year in which Peruzzi was working
under Bramante he was painting frescoes of the Life of Our
Lady in the lower half of the tribune apse of Sant' Onofrio.
Of these frescoes the *Flight into Egypt* depicts a scene of
pastoral uneventfulness which little accords with the subject
but thoroughly reflects the idyllic tastes of Pinturicchio.
Even so you will in vain scan the Tuscan town in the background for a hint of Peruzzi's architectural style so soon to
be registered. Yet five years later he was engaged upon
building in Trastevere a palace for the banker Agostino
Chigi. The façades of the Villa Farnesina are distinguished
by the familiar feature of a slim pilaster between the windows
of each storey, a conceit he had inherited from Bramante.
Nevertheless they have already lost that withdrawn, exclusive air of self-defence, and are instead welcoming and
serene. How much more so they must have appeared when
the wall spaces were still covered with historic scenes painted
by the architect—for by now Peruzzi was thoroughly under
the spell of Raphael, who rather than Bramante seems to
have aroused in him a passion for the antique. Hence-
forward he devoted his leisure to measuring remains in the
fora and the Campagna. The pretty insipidities learnt from
Pinturicchio were swiftly discarded in favour of a more
heroic style of composition. He was inspired to adorn the
villa he had built in the manner in which Ovid in the
Metamorphoses described the Palace of the Sun:

Regia solis erat sublimibus alta columnis,
Clara micante auro flammasque imitante pyropo.[2]

It was to be an amalgamation of all the arts, of which no one
was to supersede another and the workmanship was to be

---

[2] "The sun's bright palace on high columns raised
With burnished gold and flaming jewels blazed."

Joseph Addison's translation of the opening couplet of Book II of the
Metamorphoses.

more beautiful than the material—*materiam superabat opus*.[3] In fact his own part in the decoration was limited. The greater part was carried out by Raphael and his intimate band of followers, Giulio Romano, Giovanni da Udine and Francesco Penni. Thanks to the joint efforts of these men the downstairs loggia is renowned among apartments owing their decoration to a combination of genius with a spirit of devoted brotherhood. Over the band we may suppose that Raphael was the presiding genius and Peruzzi, as architect of the villa, the co-ordinator of operations.[4] The two end walls of the great saloon on the first floor are certainly his. He adorned them with distant views of the Borgo and Janiculum. Each consists of a background group of buildings seen through a large half-concealed portico such as the ancients loved. With the cunning of an accomplished painter he contrived the perspective effects needed to simulate architecture, and by means of massive foreground columns obtained an illusion of greater space than the actual dimensions of the saloon allowed.

Thenceforward the dominating art for Peruzzi was to be architecture. The process was familiar. It had happened with Bramante. It was to happen with Michelangelo. It was even to happen with our first renaissance architect, Inigo Jones, who before he adopted architecture, by which he made his name, was known as a "picture maker" and then as a masque designer. Peruzzi did not at once abandon painting but he was gradually to make it minister to the requirements of architecture. As late as 1515–17 he composed a fresco, *The Presentation in the Temple* for the Ponzetti Chapel in Santa Maria della Pace. In the conventional figures of the foreground are still discernible traces of Peruzzi's Sienese upbringing. But the perspective background is the focus of the composition. The dominating feature is a four-columned temple portico of the Ionic order, its cushioned frieze

---

[3] "The matter vied not with the sculptor's thought."
[4] Raphael's remarkable team repeated the performance a few years later at the Villa Madama. Several survivors of the team helped decorate the Palazzo Massimo many years later.

painted with the same dense foliage which he was actually to carve some four to five years later upon the frieze of the principal door of San Michele in Bosco, Bologna. The fresco is in fact more an architectural representation than a pictorial composition and interprets fairly correctly an ancient Roman temple of the Augustan age. In other words Peruzzi was by this time more completely in the grip of antiquarianism than ever Bramante had been. You may understand how much by a glance at the Doric four-columned portico of his little brick chapel outside the Porta Camollia, Siena, which is practically a reproduction of a Roman temple front and likewise dates from this period of his architectural career.

But Peruzzi was far too creative to be content with mere reproduction. Like Bramante he developed into an eclectic. By intensive study of the methods of the ancients he was enabled to evolve an architecture that was new because it was so widely derivative. More imaginative and more sensitive in the handling of detail than Bramante he achieved a greater diversity of forms which can only be apprehended by a minute scrutiny of his architecture. A characteristic example of his early eclecticism is the front of the church of La Sagra, at Carpi, where the Roman triumphal arch of the lower stage has been extended into the mediaeval clerestory arrangement of the upper, thus producing by accident or design a result which foreshadows Palladio's familiar façade motif of a pediment within a pediment, as at his Venetian church of Il Redentore. Incidentally Peruzzi anticipated Palladio in another important feature, the so-called Palladian opening. Within the courtyard of the Palazzo Medici in the Via Giulia, he provided two end loggias, or screens, consisting of the very same round arch over columns flanked by lesser flat-headed openings, which in repetitive form surround Palladio's Basilica at Vicenza. These Palladian sources are not altogether surprising when we recall that Serlio, whose volumes of *Architectura* were the inspiration of Palladio's *Quattro Libri dell' Architettura*, was Peruzzi's pupil.

The culmination of Peruzzi's eclecticism is the palace he built for Prince Pietro Massimo between 1532 and 1536, the year of the architect's death. Here you may best appreciate his astonishing sense of scale and proportion, his enrichment of plain surfaces with the minimum of extraneous ornamentation, and withal his minute regard for detail and extreme delicacy in its treatment.

The Massimo family had suffered severe hardship in the Sack of Rome of 1527 by the Constable de Bourbon. To some extent the disaster was their own fault, for, although they were the richest of the Roman princes, they were about the most parsimonious. In response to the Pope's urgent request for funds to raise troops to withstand the impending assault of the imperialist army, Prince Domenico Massimo, the then representative of the family, refused to advance a penny. The consequences to the City and the Massimo family were devastating. One of Domenico's sons, Prince Giuliano, was killed. The famous Massimo printing press, the first to have been established in Rome, was totally destroyed and the house so badly damaged that it was rendered uninhabitable. Prince Domenico, overwhelmed by his misfortunes, died of a broken heart. His three surviving sons, Pietro, Angelo and Luca, having recovered from the shock of these events and divided amongst themselves what inheritance remained to them, commissioned Peruzzi to build a new palace, or rather three adjacent palaces on fresh foundations.[5] Only Pietro's palace was finished just before Peruzzi's death, which was hastened by financial worry caused by the reluctance of the Massimi to pay him adequately. It is uncertain how far Angelo's palace, to the west of Pietro's had proceeded. Luca's, which was to have been across the road, was never begun.

The Massimi are a family of the greatest antiquity and claim descent from the patrician Fabius Maximus who in 202 B.C. had led the armies of Rome against Hannibal. Of

[5] This was explained by an inscription on the frieze of Pietro's palace, which existed when Letarouilly drew the elevation.

their origin they have long been exceedingly proud and about its authenticity correspondingly sensitive. When Napoleon interrogated one of the Massimi with that brusqueness which intimidated most people: "Is it true that you are a descendant of the Roman general?" he received the curt retort: "I cannot prove it, but the tradition has been current for over a thousand years in my family." Prince Pietro, ever mindful of his lineage and especially proud of his titles of "del Portico" and "alle Colonne" instructed Peruzzi that the design of his new house must follow a Roman model and incorporate a portico with columns. With the added injunction that the strictest economies must be observed, he then left the architect to his own devices.

The Palazzo Massimo, like many old Roman palaces, has its associations both terrible and sublime. Within the first century of its existence it earned a curse and a blessing. Prince Lelio Massimo[6] had six sons. After the death of his wife he married in 1585 a lady who in the past had incited her previous lover, the great Marcantonio Colonna, to assassinate her first husband. Prince Lelio's sons decided that they must immediately rid themselves of their new stepmother. Five of them walked into her bedroom on the day after the marriage and killed her. Their father was to die of grief but not without pronouncing a curse upon his five sons as murderers. He enacted the pythonic rôle with the utmost solemnity. Crucifix in hand he invoked the revenge of the Almighty upon them. Then embracing the youngest boy, Pompeo, who was innocent of the crime, he implored God to allow the succession of his family to be through him alone. In the sequel the five brothers met violent deaths without leaving issue, whereas Pompeo, who had declined or been too young to assist them in the murder of his stepmother, lived to perpetuate the lineage.

This distressing story is overshadowed by that of a miracle

---

[6] Lelio was the son of Prince Luca, whose house Peruzzi never built. He and his family evidently lived in part of his uncle Pietro's palace.

which took place in the house on 16th March of the previous
year. Paolo Massimo, a grandson of Prince Angelo, was a
boy of remarkable sanctity. At the age of fourteen he died
of a fever. Saint Philip Neri, a friend of his father,[7] was at
the time celebrating Mass in the city. He was instantly sent
for. When he had finished Mass, he rode post-haste to the
Palazzo Massimo, sprinkled the boy's face with holy water
and breathed upon him. Then taking his hand he miraculously brought him back to life. Paolo sat up in bed and
announced that he wished to confess one sin which he had
previously forgotten. This done the saint asked him if he
chose to remain alive or would rather yield his soul to God.
The boy after grave reflection decided to die again. "Then
go," said Saint Philip, "and pray to God for us." Whereupon
Paolo lay down and peacefully expired for the second time.
On every anniversary of that event the private chapel of the
palace built in memory of the miraculous resuscitation is
thrown open to the public. Prince Massimo's servants put
on their livery, sky blue tail coats braided with magenta
cuffs and sewn with gold buttons, magenta waistcoats,
magenta breeches and blue silk stockings, and black patent
leather shoes with gold buckles. Under the portico a major-
domo, engaged for his handsome looks, stands and welcomes
the visitors. He wears a velvet and damask coat slashed with
a garter blue ribbon, and a tricorne hat over a grey periwig,
and carries a long silver staff of office.

The site allowed on which to build the Palazzo Massimo
is as awkward as can be. Its shape is an irregular wedge.
From the street elevation, which is curved, the area recedes
into an ever narrowing extremity. Peruzzi, however, like
Wren when faced with rebuilding some of the City churches,
seemed inspired to triumph in spite of the problem presented.
His recurring difficulty was therefore how to arrive at regular
shaped rooms. This he solved, certainly to optical if not
always to structural satisfaction, by adroitly thickening

---

[7] Fabrizio, son of Prince Angelo. He had had five daughters before Paolo's
birth which was predicted by Saint Philip Neri.

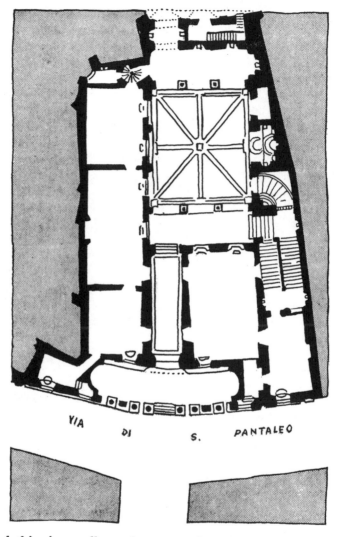

YIA   DI   S.   PANTALEO

and thinning walls, and so arranging his patterned ceilings that asymmetries might be overlooked. The result is that your eye is often happily deceived by a cunning decorative legerdemain, and right angles are far rarer than you may suppose. The plan of the palace more or less follows, in accordance with Prince Pietro's injunctions, the disposition of a patrician's house in the time of the Augustan Romans. I say more or less, because the Palazzo Massimo is by no means the slavish reproduction of the ancient domestic disposition which the guide books like to insist upon.

In the first place Peruzzi's antiquarianism could not, any more than Bramante's before him, be rigidly carried out to the letter, even to please a princely patron. In the second place, as regards the domestic buildings of the ancients it was necessarily deficient. In Peruzzi's day Pompeii and Herculaneum were still underground and Ostia had not been excavated. His only knowledge of Roman domestic architecture was gleaned from the unillustrated pages of Vitruvius. It is extraordinary that his knowledge was so advanced. All that we, fortunate in the light of subsequent discoveries, can point to in the plan of the Palazzo Massimo is a pale reflection of that of a Roman town house. To begin with, Peruzzi's endeavour to expand his wedge-shaped site, of which the wider end faces the street, into a long rectangle was governed by the Roman domestic layout. The recessed portico, which he provided to satisfy Prince Pietro's pride of title, corresponds with the *vestibulum* found in the grandest Roman houses. From it a narrow entrance passage leads to the first courtyard, which takes the place of the ancient *atrium*. The *atrium* was always open to the sky (as is of course the courtyard) by means of an inward sloping roof called a *compluvium*, through which the rain fell to be gathered by a variety of channels into a central tank. In his courtyard Peruzzi supplied against a wall a fountain and basin (since rebuilt). Immediately beyond the first courtyard he built a further passage, in the place of the Roman *tablinum*, leading to a second court, corresponding to the *peristylium* in the private quarters of an ancient residence. In other words Peruzzi followed the invariable Roman plan of a straight axis from one end of a house to the other, which enabled passers-by to look straight through from the street to the far side when the curtains at the entrance were drawn back. But beyond these somewhat general interpretations Peruzzi could not and did not go. The conventional Roman accessories of *cubicula* for visitors, *alae* and *tablinum* grouped around the *atrium*, and of *cubicula* for the family, *triclinium*, *oecus*, *pinacoteca*, *biblioteca* and *culina* grouped around the inner *peristylium* were not adhered to.[8] The mere differences in living conditions between the two civilizations would have made a faithful reproduction of the plan impossible as well as ludicrous.

To study the front of the Palazzo Massimo with thoroughness is to take your life in both hands. It can only be done from the south side of the wide Corso Vittorio Emanuele, which is a relentless inferno of roaring traffic. The pavement is hardly less perilous on account of the scurry of pedestrians. Nevertheless your only course is to flatten yourself against the south-east corner where the Corso is met by the paradoxically named Via del Paradiso. From no other spot can you with safety see both ends of the front at the same time. Directly in your central line of vision, however, is a thick junction of trolley-bus wires. Overcoming this interruption by a process of stretching and lowering yourself you may admire the clean lines of the rusticated elevation of grim, grey travertine, only slightly smudged here and there by the vicissitudes of over four centuries. You may not at once notice that the front is curved to follow the contour of the original street, named the Via di San Pantaleo, which was far narrower than the widened Corso. Peruzzi did his utmost by clever adjustment of spaces to subordinate the unavoidable convexity which was dictated to him. There exists in the Uffizi a preliminary design in which the palace elevation is shown to be straight. It had necessarily to be scrapped. Unlike the later baroque architects who positively delighted

[8] *Vestibulum* = entrance hall: *atrium* = hall: *compluvium* = quadrangular open space in the middle of a house towards which the roofs sloped: *tablinum* = archive room, or balcony: *peristylium* = court surrounded by columns: *cubicula* = bedrooms: *alae* = colonnades: *triclinium* = dining-room: *oecus* = saloon: *pinacoteca* = picture gallery: *biblioteca* = library: *culina* = kitchen.

in any excuse for a curve, Peruzzi here attempted, fairly
successfully, to distract the eye from it. The next thing you
will notice with the help of the plan (page 88) is the effort he
made to feign width of site by encroaching upon the façade
of the neighbouring palace, Prince Angelo's, to the extent
of one window bay, comprising a small room behind. He
furthermore accentuated the nobility of his front by continuing the line of coupled portico columns with a bay of
coupled pilasters on either side. The restricted width of the
site was a serious handicap to splendour as you can tell by
the careful manipulation of planes to which the architect
had recourse. The ground storey is an ingenious adaptation
of the old Pantheon theme of altar recesses. The two
pilastered bays flanking the portico carry on the theme
across the whole front and yet allow some much required
rooms overlooking the street. In fact the inclusion of the
columned portico, the second of Prince Pietro's conditions,
must have been no small embarrassment to the architect
obliged to supply all the accommodation he could. As it was,
the portico could only be recessed owing to the narrowness
of the original street. In spite of these difficulties Peruzzi
managed to provide a suitably wide intercolumn for a grand
entrance.

Apart from the vertical columns and pilasters all the
emphasis of the façade is strictly horizontal. You see it
neatly underlined by the clean sweep of the platform, now
foreshortened by one step as a result of the raised pavement
level. You see it continued by the shallow caps of columns
and pilasters and deeply underscored by the pronounced
entablature they carry. Above are three rows of seven
windows and crowning the whole face like a clean gash
against the sky a cornice of far-reaching projection which
Michelangelo thought fit to copy on the Palazzo Farnese.
The great delicacy and variety of moulds under the upper
cornice cannot properly be appreciated from the ground and
may best be admired in the wonderfully detailed drawings
of Paul Letarouilly. The windows of the piano nobile

have lintels carried on brackets and projecting bases (suggested by the tabernacle features inside the Pantheon) which give shadow and movement. These windows retain a flavour of quattrocento goldsmith's work and may be a legacy of Pinturicchio's schooling. The windows of the second and third floors are unusual in that they are of the scale of mezzanine windows; the surrounds of those on the second floor are carved in strapwork scrolls, commonly found on Genoese but rarely on Roman palaces. All the windows preserve their original casements and octagonal panes.

To step from the pavement straight into the portico for the first time is an unforgettable experience of good architecture. There are no railings, no gate, no physical barriers of any kind to prevent you turning aside from bedlam into one of the most exquisite creations of the European Renaissance. There you may sit upon the travertine benches whose cabriole legs and pawed feet are marvels of carving in a most intractable material. The area of the portico is a very small segment decorated in the grandest manner conceivable to civilized man. The columns of the portico are reflected by pilasters on the inner curved wall, which like the façade presents a rusticated surface. Critics have pointed out the anomaly of Roman Doric columns having Attic bases and capitals, and complained that Peruzzi who never visited Greece was introducing motifs which he did not properly understand. But surely the final criterion of a technical anomaly is whether its effect is absurd or sublime. There can be no other. In this case only a curmudgeon will argue that the firm profiles of bases and capitals and the sharp, thin and unusually projecting *abacus* (the upper member of each capital) are offensive and a mistake. Now look at the two ground floor windows under the portico which you find in no sense incongruous. The derivation of their clean and distinct moulds is quite clearly from Roman Republican date and their prototypes are to be found, for example, upon the Tomb of Bibulus in the Piazza di Venezia. In other words

Peruzzi had complete confidence in his purposeful eclecticism. The whole conception of the portico is unorthodox and yet is none the worse for it. You may almost say it has pictorial flavour rather than architectural reality. And this leads me to suggest that Peruzzi was indeed reproducing in architecture a design which he had already adumbrated in fresco, namely upon the end walls of the upstairs saloon in the Farnesina, where the columns have the same distinctive profiles and the curved colonnades are even finished with niches for statues.

Here the niches, features of undeniable beauty, have plaster half-domes worked in lozenge panels of allegorical figures taken—and we come upon yet another anomaly—from Roman tomb work of the first or second centuries A.D. One wonders this time where Peruzzi can have found his inspiration, from what particular tomb or catacomb on the Via Latina, now possibly destroyed. For sure enough the very same conventional figures in plaster are to be seen on the vault of the underground Basilica di Porta Maggiore which in the sixteenth century was entirely unknown and was only brought to light within the last forty years. Within each niche a figure most regrettably chipped and dirty—the torso on the right is an antique—stands on a Roman plinth. The ribs of the deeply coffered portico ceiling bear a flat mould of tentative Greek key pattern. The very same key pattern is found upon the underneath of the arch leading to the Chigi Chapel in Santa Maria del Popolo, which is supposed to have been designed by Raphael, and may even have been built by Peruzzi, for their old banker patron, the owner of the Farnesina. The rectangular plaster panels deeply sunk within the ribs are in patterns of lyres and honeysuckles which likewise owe their provenance to Greece. The middle panel is reserved for a shield of the Massimo arms. The richness of design and delicacy of detail in this ceiling are unsurpassed in renaissance Rome.

The great doorway is centralized on the curved wall opposite the widest intercolumn. It is one of Peruzzi's most

happy acts of bravura. It must be compared with his marble
doorway of San Michele in Bosco. Like the other it is slightly
diminished towards the lintel in the classical Greek manner,
and is distinguished by a bold frieze of laurel leaves and
acorns. To the very rich entablature Peruzzi has added
modillion blocks, which in the Doric order are quite
unorthodox but nevertheless lend welcome support to the
projecting cornice.

The doorway takes you down the brick paved passage
which corresponds to that which led from the *vestibulum* of a
Roman dwelling. Four wooden doors with large lion heads
within circular panels give on to the passage. The overdoors
are raised into roundels for busts, framed by naked terminal
figures holding scrolls. Such a florid design is uncommon
to the High Renaissance, but characteristic of Peruzzi's
individualism. It marks a distinct break from the almost
sedate decorative designs of Bramante. You will probably
recognize the influence which these doors and door cases
exerted upon Venetian architects of the late sixteenth
century, an influence which furthermore descended to the
French rococo decorators of the reigns of Louis XIV and
Louis XV.

From a cornice of many moulds springs a rounded vault
in stucco of the finest quality. The much vaunted stucco
work of the Italian Renaissance is seldom as refined as it
became in the hands of English and Irish plaster-workers of
the eighteenth century. But here, as upon the half-domes
of the portico, it attains a quality only matched by the Latin
stuccoists of the tombs and by Giovanni da Udine in the
loggias of the Vatican and the Villa Madama. Indeed the
vault was in all probability the work of da Udine. It is
framed within a border of little rams' heads, the curled
horns weighted with heavy swags. A central panel portrays a
triumphal chariot laden with martial trophies and drawn by
a mounted elephant in honour of the exploits of Fabius
Maximus. Peruzzi delighted in designing bas-reliefs in the
antique manner when he could not come by original ones.

Over the entrances to the Villa Farnesina and the Palazzo Medici he was able to insert ancient reliefs which he had gleaned from strewn fragments in the Campagna.

Since the courtyard is an imperfect rectangle the inner colonnade where you now emerge is not properly related to it. The dimensions of the colonnade are curiously awry and the plan has no right angles. Nevertheless, these defects are skilfully overcome by adjustment of the vaulting panels, which induce a make-believe symmetry. From the first bay of the vault, so as to be seen from the street, hangs a brass and bronze lantern of much beauty. It is in the form of a Doric columned altar supported in the air by winged lions, their extremities gathered into a ring. The top of the altar sprouts tongues of flame. The elevations of the courtyard are in that Hellenistic style most favoured by Peruzzi, a style evolved during the last era of the Roman Republic at Tivoli and Palestrina, where he had ample opportunities of studying it.

The rectangular openings above the entablature of the colonnade are so ungainly that you may well wonder if Peruzzi can have been responsible for them. They were of course inserted to afford more light to the passage below. In consequence the beautiful plaster panels of the vaults are mutilated in a very horrible manner. Peruzzi was, however, addicted to perforating his friezes with windows. He did so very discreetly on the façades of the Farnesina and thereby led Sansovino to follow suit on the Library of San Marco, Venice. The oblique method of lighting the chapels in the Pantheon by means of openings in the attic storey—a method which there is legitimate and unexceptionable—may have suggested itself to him, or he may even have found a precedent in Mantegna's fresco, *The Baptism of Hermogenes* in the Eremitani at Padua. We cannot tell. All we can say is that the result is a warning how an unorthodox innovation, even from the hand of genius, may prove unsuccessful.

Aware of the inordinate depth and narrowness of his courtyard-well Peruzzi contrived that the best view of it

95

should be had from the first floor loggia.[9] This is approached from the inner colonnade by a barrel vaulted staircase in one short and two long and narrow flights. Oddly enough the staircase is the only feature of the palace to which Vasari specifically referred—"It deserves the utmost commendation," he wrote—and yet to my mind it is not particularly remarkable. You may admire the groined vault of the top landing as seen from the loggia through the round-headed doorway, whose arch is adorned with a chain moulding. The highly decorated roundels for busts belong to a later date.[10]

By now Peruzzi very sensibly abandoned all pretence of following a Roman model. Indeed how could he do otherwise, for nowhere in Italy was he able to look for an archetype? Instead, he gave rein to that original invention of which a great artist of the Italian Renaissance was capable. His loggia and the large saloon to which it leads are among the most exquisite creations of this golden age. Alas, that the painted loggia is allowed to fall into decay and the saloon (which anyway is not available to the public) has lately been deprived of its contents and some of its ornamental features!

For the first time we find an alternative architectural order to the Doric introduced. The upper stage of the courtyard is Ionic. The columns and pilasters of the loggia, with their marked swelling and neat little capitals, are of Hellenic proportions. The columns are wrought of verde antique, their capitals and bases and the pilasters being rendered in a white veined marble. Within the three wall bays are a double door of oak, minutely carved with raised oval panels and strips of fruit and flowers, and a pair of landscape frescoes within highly ornate *trompe l'oeil* frames.

The ceiling of the loggia is typical of the cinquecento. Being low the compartments have been made fairly shallow.

[9] Beyond this courtyard is a second, corresponding to the Roman *peristylium*.
[10] The niches, containing antique busts, were designed by G. Battista Solari, in 1610. He was a stuccoist and also made the present charming fountain. His work is recognizably coarser than Peruzzi's.

The oak ribs are carved with a chain mould, and frame rectangles and hexagons tightly packed with conventional floral motifs. The Massimo escutcheon within a wreath is proudly displayed upon a central panel. All the enrichments are gilded against a chequered ground. It was Italian ceilings such as this which were imitated in France and England during the reigns of Francis I and Henry VIII. Unfortunately their popularity in the northern countries endured but a short time and too soon succumbed before the influence of ponderous and vulgarized versions from the Netherlands and Germany.

The Roman Renaissance was the first era in history to concentrate upon elegant conditions of domestic living. For examples of splendid apartments you must, however, visit the Palazzo Farnese, Peruzzi's own Villa Farnesina, the Villa Madama and the Palazzo Colonna. The interiors of these palaces and villas excel as masterpieces of the decorative arts, with which we are not primarily concerned here. The architecture of the Palazzo Massimo is not so majestic as that of several other princely dwellings, such as the Palazzo Borghese and Palazzo Cancellaria, nor even so fanciful as the Palazzo Spada or the Villa di Papa Giulio. You may accordingly wonder why I have made it my choice in a study of Roman domestic architecture of the Renaissance. It is never easy to justify a personal predilection. Admittedly the Palazzo Massimo has little that is monumental to offer. It may not take the breath away at a first glance. It makes few concessions to casual acquaintance. It is in fact almost unassuming. Having said as much I contend that its beauties have to be sought and investigated before they can be fully appreciated. They are not obvious but subtle. They rely on absolutely no adventitious decorative aids to popularity. The Palazzo Massimo is an immaculate, aristocratic little building in consequence. It is exclusively architectural. It is, I firmly believe, the very epitome of domestic architecture in the purest and least affected of styles.

97

BIBLIOGRAPHY

W. J. Anderson & A. Stratton. *The Architecture of the Renaissance in Italy*, 1927

P. M. Letarouilly. *Edifices de Rome Moderne*, 1840–57.

Luigi Càllari. *I Palazzi di Roma*, 1932.

Giorgio Vasari. Baldassare Peruzzi, in *Lives of the Painters*, Vol. III, Mrs. Foster's trs. 1887.

Enciclopedia Italiana. Peruzzi, Baldassare.

W. W. Kent. *Life and Works of B. Peruzzi*, New York, 1925.

R. Lanciani. *Golden Days of the Renaissance in Rome*, 1906.

F. W. Bedford. Articles on Peruzzi in *R.I.B.A. Journal*, Nov. 1901 and Oct. 1902.

J. H. Worthington. Peruzzi, *R.I.B.A. Journal*, Oct. 1913.

Professor Aitchisons. Article on Peruzzi, *R.I.B.A. Journal*, Aug. 1901.

G. G. Rossi. Life and Works of B. Peruzzi, *R.I.B.A. Sessional Papers*, 1870–1.

Percier et Fontaine. *Palais, Maisons—Rome*, 1798.

Conte Pompeo Litta—*Famiglie Celebri Italiane*, 1837.

Note: Since the above account was written, thirty-three years ago, the Palazzo Massimo has fallen into a very sorry condition. The author is assured that it is about to be restored to its pristine condition.

BAROQUE I

―――⸺⊂⊃∘◉∘⊂⸺―――

Sant' Andrea Al Quirinale

THE site of this church on the highest of the seven hills of Rome is a generous one. It is not cramped but open. It occupies a recess of the wide, straight Via del Quirinale and faces north-west. On one side of it are some public gardens and on the other the spacious grounds of the Jesuit seminary to which it is attached. In front of it stretches like a long yawn the dull, respectable front of the Quirinal Palace. The district is isolated, elevated, irreproachable and, for Rome, comparatively quiet. Since the street is not a commercial one the traffic is infrequent and swift.

The first thing to bear in mind is that Sant' Andrea was built for the Jesuits, a religious society which is perhaps unique in believing that the greatest material sumptuousness may be commensurable with the strictest spiritual discipline. Accordingly the church was designed to conform to palatial standards in so far as prodigality of decoration was concerned, notwithstanding that the scale was small. Today Sant' Andrea still retains a flavour of distinct well-being and an air of courtly grooming. Professor Lanciani held a rather improbable theory that the foundations of the church were dug to the order of Urban VIII in 1644, which was the year of that Pope's death. At all events nothing further was done for at least fourteen years by which time Urban's successor, Innocent X, had reigned and gone. On 26th October, 1658, approval for actual building to start was formally granted by Pope Alexander VII and on 3rd November the first stone was laid. The expense was entirely borne by an enormously wealthy nephew of the late Pope Innocent, Prince Camillo Pamphili, who until his recent unorthodox marriage with the heiress of the Aldobrandini family, had been a cardinal. The architect from first to last was Bernini. In 1658 he was just sixty years old.

Gian Lorenzo Bernini was a Neapolitan by birth but a Roman by adoption. Although a handful of his churches and villas are to be found sprinkled about the towns of the Campagna, his work is practically confined to Rome, which since his early youth was his permanent home and centre. There he remained throughout his long life, only once leaving it with great reluctance for a tiresome and abortive visit to Paris. This was made at the urgent request of Louis XIV who ultimately rejected the designs for the Louvre which he had prepared for the King with much care and trouble. He was the first exclusive Roman to become in his lifetime an architect of international renown. Bramante, Peruzzi and Michelangelo contributed as largely as he to the Roman Renaissance, but they had left important buildings in the other parts of Italy whence they sprang and only drifted to Rome in their maturity. Bernini whose architecture crystalized the ideals of his age and gave expression to the whole seicento, confined his immense talents to enhancing the splendour of individual popes and embellishing a single city. Yet so macrocosmic were the seven hills of Rome and so overwhelming was Bernini's personality that the style he evolved soon spread to the remotest confines of Christendom and raised a new tide in architectural taste. It was as though in Georgian England Thomas Paty of Bristol or John Wood of Bath (two cities scarcely smaller in population than Rome of the seventeenth century) developed a manner of building so compulsive that it radiated across this island and the Continent an influence far-reaching and disturbing.

What was the secret of Bernini's influence? All his life the man was pre-eminently a sculptor. As such he had been schooled in his youth. He never really became what we call a professional architect, nor had he been apprenticed to a master architect. In so far as a giant can resemble a pigmy Bernini may be compared to his English contemporary Nicholas Stone, who was schooled as a sculptor, excelled as a sculptor and produced buildings which were in truth sculptural rather than architectural. The difference between the buildings of each is of course that Stone's were merely the tentative essays of a provincial mason whereas Bernini's were the confident expressions of a universal genius. It is forceful personality as much as executive ability which can create a new mode of art and impress it upon a whole era. Bernini possessed both these qualities in overflowing measure. Look at the man's portraits and see the nervous force behind his spare figure. The massive head is like an anvil from which when the intellect strikes sparks of invention fly in all directions. The abundant dark hair, which in old age became snow white, is cut short. Under thick brows the eyes are deep set, vivacious and penetrating. The smouldering gaze indicates a temperament of gunpowder ready to explode with anger at the slightest provocation. It was said that one look would command the most recalcitrant to obedience. The chin, which is cleft, indicates aggressiveness. One can well understand how his volcanic and abrupt speech was accompanied by the most violent and sometimes alarming gestures.

It would be a foolish mistake to suppose that Bernini deliberately set about to break with traditional classical methods and inaugurate a new style of art to be designated the "Baroque." Doubtless he never consciously intended to go further than interpret the classical canons of art in the free manner that suited his peculiar temperament. The term Baroque, like the terms Mannerism and Rococo, is a posthumous fiction invented by art historians to make their self-imposed task easier. Historic labels which have little enough significance for posterity have absolutely no meaning whatever to the participants of history. As it happened, Bernini like his great predecessors of the Renaissance was a devoted student of the antique, actually a restorer of ancient sculpture, and (in spite of his share, which may have been indirect, in the spoliation of the Pantheon bronze work) a passionate lover of ancient architecture.

The development of Bernini's art is easily followed through graduated stages. There are the allegorical sculpture groups and figures of his early youth, the Daphne and Apollo, the Rape of Proserpine, the David slinging a catapult, wherein a striving towards the looseness and sinuosity of his maturer work is accompanied by an insipidity which does not immediately accord with our notion of the artist's temperament. To some extent the sacred figures of Bernini's later life never entirely lost this touch of insipidity which was the result of too uncontrolled a projection of emotion into his work. If his Daphne is too virginal and his David too self-righteous, his Saint Teresa transfixed by the arrow of Divine Love is too ecstatic to be absolutely convincing. "Love touched her heart" the poet wrote of this "undaunted daughter of desires," "and lo! it beats High, and burns with such brave heats."[1] There is also something a little shocking to our prosaic notions of mysticism in the victim "kissing the sweetly-killing dart." We find the fervour of her Divine Love embarrassing. We do not altogether believe in its sincerity. Bernini's portrait busts on the contrary are incomparable in their sincerity. The power behind them is no less forceful and is more evenly diffused. The self-indulgent, brazen and bounderish Cardinal Scipione Borghese, and the bland, easy-going, abstracted Innocent X are penetrating appraisals of human beings which no sculptor but Michelangelo among the moderns has equalled. Since we are an essentially cynical generation we can accept these portrayals of human beings in high places as natural and just.

The baroque quality of the allegorical sculpture groups is, however, not transmitted to Bernini's early buildings. Santa Bibiana (1625) is one of these. In its sedate façade there is little indication of the "movement" and straining for effects of light and shade which we associate with his name. Rather we see just another correct, flat, uninspired composition of straight lines, which is characteristic of the

[1] Richard Crashaw's *Hymn to the Name and Honour of the Admirable Saint Teresa.*

façades of his predecessors, such as Ammanati, Domenica Fontana and del Soria. Their architecture had expressed the rigid, straight-laced attitude of the Counter-Reformation, wary and stern after the religious convulsions of the previous generation. By the seventeenth century Catholic Rome could afford to relax a little and there took place a reconciliation between Counter-Reformation asceticism and that pagan hedonism, which had originally characterized renaissance humanism. Michelangelo had already tried to free architecture of the High Renaissance from the restrictions imposed by Vitruvianism, but his was a loud voice crying unheeded in the wilderness. His style was too daring and individual to be emulated by his contemporaries, especially in the papal city. Besides it conflicted with the return to discipline after the setback of the Reformation and lesser artists had neither the intrepidity nor the impulse to go against the spirit of their time. Consequently the mannerism of Michelangelo was premature and shortlived. But if his contemporaries were unresponsive, his seventeenth-century successors were attentive to the reverberation of his message, which was to abandon tame archaeology and return to pure art. They learnt from him to think for themselves and express their own thoughts in the freedom of form. By then it was safe for them to do so. The Counter-Reformation was over. The Catholic Church was once more settled down within its reduced empire. It resorted to new methods of winning and keeping the faith of its flock. It decided that a display of splendour and magnificence would have a wider, stronger appeal than exiguity and gloom. The Roman Church of the seventeenth century turned its attention to the spiritual welfare of the masses instead of confining it to that of the rulers. It had learnt a lesson from the leaders of the Reformation, for Luther, Zwingli and Calvin had captured the sympathies of the multitude. So its policy ceased to be esoteric and became exoteric. A changed taste was subtly infused into the fabric of new places of worship by the baroque architects who were mindful of the words of an early renaissance pope: "To create solid and stable convictions in the minds of uncultured peoples there must be something that appeals to the eye."

These cunning tactics were first adopted by the Jesuits. They began by contriving to make the interior of the Gesù church resemble in its gorgeous chapels of lapis and precious stones, its candelabra of gold, its painted ceilings and chandeliers of crystal, the heavenly mansion of the ordinary man's prayers. Here at any time of the day and night the poorest inhabitant of the meanest back street could come and bask in the palatial glitter of splendour—free of charge. It was his for the seeking. It was his foretaste in this world of a certain recompense in the next; and the more often he visited it the more certain, so he was assured, would his eternal reward be. The success of the strategy manifested inside the Gesù was repeated by the Jesuits in and outside Sant' Ignazio. This time they concentrated upon the façade a degree of that splendour to be found within. It was all strangely sensuous and theatrical. The Church seemed to be deliberately appealing to those instincts of men which hitherto had to be indulged in the profane world often on the sly. With an inclination towards architectural extravagance went an intense love of ceremonial processions and pompous vestments, and of mystical statuary of an erotic and suggestive nature.

Bernini's temperament corresponded admirably with this triumphant and joyous phase of the Church's history. He never again designed a façade so static and prim as that of Santa Bibiana. Instead he broke away from straight lines and favoured curves. At the same time—and this is a notable factor of his architecture—he never altogether departed from a correctness of manner in the outsides of his buildings. Unlike Borromini he did not twist and distort his façades into multiple sinuosities. Such antics he reserved for his interiors, where he gave free rein to his imagination. In this respect he resembled Michelangelo who is described as a mannerist rather than a full blown baroquist. Bernini revived the indoor playful spirit which had first been kindled by and was then extinguished with Michelangelo as though there had never been a gap of a hundred years between their working lives. Basically his façades were Augustan classical. His Palazzo Chigi (now Odeschalchi) before its alteration and his unexecuted design for the Louvre (which incidentally determined the design of the Versailles elevations and the south front of Chatsworth) were frankly Michelangelesque in their façades of independent basement and two storeys within one order of pilasters, and even in such details as tabernacle windows and balconied portico. His theme of Saint Peter's colonnades was just as correctly classical, consisting in a loggia crowned with an attic. Of course we call the colonnades baroque because they are curved. In other words, if, and only if, Bernini could make a curve do the same work as well as a straight line, then he would assuredly do so.

In Bernini's interiors his sculptural forms merge with his architectural contours. Architecture and sculpture become so interfused that often you ask yourself where one begins and the other ends. The question constantly arises with his tombs and reredoses where rocks and even clouds sink and float into walls, and tasselled and embroidered draperies of multi-coloured marbles form part of the structural background of his compositions. Bernini called these effects "cose naturali" and despised the French for not appreciating them. They are often scenic and stupendous, and never before in history had architecture flaunted so audaciously pictorial a tendency. One of the first essays in this new realistic manner was the baldaquin in Saint Peter's, a structure sculptural and essentially theatrical. It can hardly qualify as architecture. It is like some fantastic arabesque design found upon a tapestry. In spite of its solid bronze and preposterous weight, upon which the guide books love to dwell, it hardly seems substantial at all. The *ombrello* of involuted curves draped with a fringed pelmet is so full of "movement" that you fancy the gentlest draught through the cathedral will set it flapping. This is a joke, a cheat, you will complain. It is not architecture; it is not fair, nor right. But since it is extremely sympathetic and delightful, what does the gentle deception matter? Besides, in contriving this piece of make-believe for Pope Urban VIII Bernini retained his profound respect for tradition. In its transparency he ensured that a through view of the basilica should not be interrupted. In its shape he even followed the old Constantinian tabernacle which had stood over the same site upon eight marble columns, twisted as his four bronze columns are.

Of all the eight popes whom he served Urban VIII was the one most after his heart. Urban's impulsiveness, ruthlessness and munificence matched his own. As patron and artist the two made a formidable combination which endured for almost twenty years. Urban's reign coincided with the years of Bernini's early manhood, and helped establish his fame throughout Europe. In 1637 the artist was commissioned to make the bust of Charles I from Vandyke's triple portrait. In 1644, the year of Urban's death, John Evelyn wrote in his Roman diary that of all the modern sculptors and architects Bernini was held in the highest esteem. He had, Evelyn wrote, "a little before my coming to the city [given] a public opera . . . wherein he painted the scenes, cut the statues, invented the engines, composed the music, writ the comedy, and built the theatre." Versatility could hardly go further. After Urban's death Bernini's ties with the papacy were never again quite so intimate. Under Innocent X he was temporarily eclipsed by Borromini, but on the accession of Alexander VII in 1655 was officially reinstated, and did not look back. It was under this Pope that he began again to build churches.

So we return to Sant' Andrea al Quirinale. It is, rather surprisingly, the only church in Rome built by Bernini from the foundations. His work at Santa Bibiana was a rehabilitation of a fifth-century structure: at Santa Maria del Popolo an internal rearrangement of a church which had been aggrandized throughout the ages: and at Saint Peter's a matter of occasional redecoration, albeit covering vast areas of a vaster whole. It is undeniable that at Saint Peter's his decoration does not accord happily with the Counter-Reformation architecture. The sinuous lines (I repeat that they are not to be found on Bernini's exteriors) of his baldaquin, the broken contours of his Apostle's Chair, the swashbuckling gestures of his saints within the piers of the dome and the naturalistic detail of his monuments, powerful and emotional though they be, look grotesquely ill at ease against the austere background. Bernini cannot have been unaware of the anomaly. At Sant' Andrea on the other hand he was able to supply the architectural background to his own incomparable decoration. Consequently there are no discrepancies of style, no incongruities. The building is a harmonious whole, as complete today as when the architect left it, a perfectly integrated specimen of a Roman baroque church. No wonder that Bernini considered it the most satisfying of all his architectural works and in his old age repeatedly visited it in order to rest there from his labours and pray.

The outside is a rhythmical play of convex and concave curves governed by a vertical chord of deliberate straight lines. There is about it nothing discordant or offensive to strike the classical purist as unorthodox. From the street you may sense the complete oval of the church's plan. There is the ellipse of the central drum in hard yellow brick with its entablature in stone. The last is broken forward at intervals into an abutment whence an enormous console scroll, reminding you of those giant ones of the Salute in Venice, plants a clenched fist upon a lower outer ellipse containing the chapels. The two ellipses are spliced together by the vertical façade of a single Corinthian order in travertine. Judged by itself the façade might be the frontispiece to a temple of the Empire. It is straight with the street, its correct pediment carried by pilasters, duplicated at the angles and ingeniously returned so that the entablature is carefully married to that of the oval drum. The strong, punctuating chord of straight lines is what preserves the

strict classicality of the whole building. But hereafter
Bernini again indulges in his favourite curves. Under a
massive window, in shape more than a semicircle and
almost a horseshoe, is a convex portico of the Ionic order,
which adroitly carries on the order of the chapel ellipse.
Young James Gibbs, the future architect of St. Mary-le-
Strand, called it "a masterpiece of art" and the memory of
it may even have lingered in his mind when he designed the
ambitious baroque portico of that island church. The portico
of Sant' Andrea is carried by columns so set that their
capitals and pedestals follow the curve of the hood. This is
surmounted by a broken pediment from the scrolls of which
swags are deftly looped to a slightly tilted escutcheon bearing
the Pamphili arms under a coronet. In spite of the hardness of
the travertine the carving is wonderfully crisp and delicate,
as indeed it would have been if the material available had
been iron ore, for never were the renaissance craftsmen in
the least deterred by their materials from achieving the
artistic purpose they had in view. From the portico columns
shallow steps descend in a gentle ripple of semicircles and
lose themselves in the level of the pavement. To complete the
astonishing effect of movement Bernini extended the façade
by two quadrants of a retaining wall, curved and panelled,
which end in portals with swan-necked pediments. The
concave forecourt outlined by the quadrants was the result
of some consideration, for in a first plan the architect had
intended to enclose the front of the church within a rectangular court which would have detracted from the convexity of
its ellipse. As it is, the result attained is an echo of that
vaster scheme of embracing colonnades which Bernini had
already conceived but not yet added to the façade of Saint
Peter's.

Now you pass under the half-dome of the portico and
walk inside. Space, colour, splendour and opulence are
what strike you immediately. The air of palatial well-being
is most marked. Few are the lesser churches of Rome, or even
Italy which, however lavish their original decoration, are

Palazzo Massimo Alle Colonne

Palazzo Massimo – plaster vault panel

maintained in a manner suitable to it. Here all is garnished and shining. It is seldom that you miss the ageing acolyte in a black satinet jacket, idly flicking the altar rails with a feather brush or nonchalantly sweeping fragments of dust off the polychrome floor into a pan with a long handle. For the floor has the polished surface of a looking-glass radiating colours. Grey and white marble ribs follow the pattern of the ceiling. Under the lantern a central oval frames the gorgeous achievement of Cardinal Spinola in *giallo antico* with two supporters in mosaic holding funerary scrolls. A *putto* seated beside an overturned hour-glass and a skull waves a broken sieve in evidence of the mortality even of a prince of the Church. At your feet the proud shield of Cardinal Sforza Pallavicino lies between the fat, dangling tassels of his scarlet hat, all in porphyry, and an inscription in *Siena* and *verde antique*. In front of the sanctuary is a third armorial display in honour of Cardinal Camillo Miltius Michiolantinsi even more magnificent, with inlays of porphyry, *siena*, *cottonello* and black marbles. It consists of a spread eagle on a shield with supporters of Justice and Prudence holding a mirror. These memorials are late seventeenth-century additions and their flamboyant designs and heraldic colours enhance the baroque splendour of the interior. The walls, entirely filmed with marble, reflect the sunlight thrown down from the lantern above. The marble is Cottanello, or Sicilian jasper found in the quarries near Moricone, Sabina. It is brown-red, flecked and streaked with white, recalling the colour and suggesting the consistency of raspberry fool. The Corinthian pilasters and entablature, all but the frieze, are by contrast in white marble dashed with grey. White, too, are the marble and stucco figures against the rich, almost oppressive gold canopy of the dome.

Whereas the Counter-Reformation churches adhered to the severely rectangular, or old basilican plan, the seicento churches tended to revert to the central plan of the early Renaissance. The first baroque architect to build to this formula was Pietro da Cortona at San Luca in 1640. He adopted the Greek cross plan and placed columns against the undulating walls of the interior with niches between them in an endeavour to catch contrasting lights and shadows. Borromini thirteen years later developed the same theme at Sant' Agnese in Agone, by providing deeply recessed chapels in the arms, and Bernini in a second church he built for Pope Alexander at Castel Gandolfo did likewise. But at Sant' Andrea his choice of the ellipse was a plan entirely novel.

The narthex was a feature upon which renaissance architects were most insistent. They paid great attention to first impressions and they wished a visitor on entering an interior to view it exactly right. They believed that he must not be plunged straightway into it if he was properly to appreciate its proportions. Instead he must be allowed a pause to view it as distantly as possible. Robert Adam understood the meaning of this theory when he provided a narrow screened passageway, or narthex, at the main entrance end of the great hall at Kedleston. Bernini had written that on entering a curved church a man naturally advanced seven or eight paces before taking up a stance and looking about him, since his first instinct was to get clear of the doorway. Therefore he advocated what he called "un piccolo corpo sporgente" into which the visitor could step and from which he might take a detached view of the proportions of the interior. So here at Sant' Andrea Bernini arranged that you should walk straight into the first large recess, which he purposely made shallower and, by omitting flanking coupled columns, wider than its opposite fellow. In other words by sacrificing symmetry he contrived that you should have as uninterrupted a view as possible of the whole church as though you were standing outside it. This then is the proper stance that you should adopt for your preliminary survey.

You will soon understand why the sense of space is so apparent when you realize your position within the narthex recess. Unlike San Carlo alle Quattro Fontane where the entrance is at one of the sharp ends of an elliptical plan and

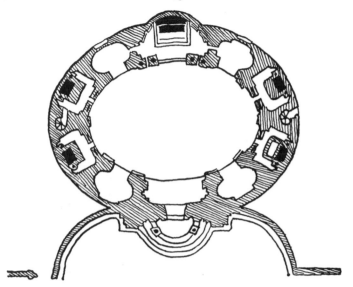

so offers the visitor a long perspective vista, Sant' Andrea has
the entrance placed at one of the two most obtuse points of
the ellipse, in face of the high altar which is at its closest
opposite. You will in fact step straight from the narthex into
the body of the church which stretches on either side of you.
Your eye at a glance will take in the church's greatest width
and greatest expanse of dome. Confronting you within the
opposite recess is the sanctuary which you will notice to be
enshrined in light, whereas the remaining chapels are
subdued by shadow. This arrangement is intentional and
accords with the Jesuit theatrical principle that the high
altar should be the focal point of eyes and hearts. Everything
has been done to accentuate its pre-eminence by dramatic
management and enrichment.

The sanctuary is formed by two pairs of fluted Corinthian
columns of solid Cottanello marble brought slightly forward
from the oval circumference of the nave. The crisply carved
capitals as well as the pedestals are of grey marble. The
columns carry a heavy projecting entablature which is a

continuation of that of the curved drum. Within the returned and broken apex of the pediment the agonized figure of Saint Andrew in Carara emerges from a cloud in the same material. It is designed to balance that other typically Berninian composition over the entrance which consists of two winged figures, one with a trumpet the other an enormous flowing scroll, and both proclaiming with much gusto Camillo Pamphili's benefaction. In the sanctuary and over the altar is the most theatrical and so most baroque feature of the interior. An immense picture by Borgognone of the patron saint's crucifixion is framed in Cottanello marble and tilted forward. The top of the frame is marvellously prevented from falling over by the too delicate hands of angels in flight, whose agitated wing hover across the flanking pilasters. A host of lesser angels or *putti*—it is difficult to determine which they are—play about a bronze sheaf of golden sunbeams and flutter like a flock of pigeons around the cupola, which sheds a flood of natural light upon the high altar. This ingenious theatrical device was repeated for the setting of Saint Teresa's ecstasy in Santa Maria della Vittoria.

The side chapels are uniformly ranged under round-headed arches. They contain religious pictures in gold or Siena frames over emblems of the dove and olive branch of the Pamphili. The chapel to the left of the sanctuary shelters within a shrine of gold and lapis the mortal remains of Saint Stanislas Kostka, a noble Polish youth who renounced society and shut himself up in the adjacent college, saying, "I am not born for the good things of this world; what my heart desires are the good things of eternity." A picture by Carlo Maratta depicts the saint bathing his breast, inflamed with the agony of divine love. The devout boy died aged eighteen in 1568.

In an upstairs chapel (the Camera de S. Stanislas Kostka) he can be seen lying on his deathbed, the recumbent effigy and tomb by Pietro Legros. Clad in a loose robe of black marble the head, hands and feet are of white Carrara. The white pillows are braided; the mattress is of *giallo antico,* the red striped valance of *alabastro da Palambara.,* the platform on which the bed rests being of Egyptian alabaster, or onyx. Everything is done by the *custode* to prevent you paying your respects to this sumptuous and ravishing piece of polychrome sculpture. Do not be deterred.

The masterpiece of the interior is of course the dome. After the manner of the Pantheon dome it covers the whole area of the nave. Ever thickening ribs, like the downward strokes of a quill, descend through the shallow drum upon the entablature and fall into line above the white pilasters. Between them hexagonal coffers in white and gold diminish in size towards the lantern. Relief from the concentrated richness is given by a range of large and small windows in the drum. The large windows have heavy segmental heads crested with shells. Upon the broken pediments draped figures in Carrara marble are reclining. They are handsome youths in lively attitudes, talking to each other over their shoulders, pointing and gesticulating. Still more profane are the playful groups of chubby *putti,* some hauling at, others swinging upon loops of a heavy garland of fruit suspended the whole way round the drum from each window. Overhead, angels in stucco are seen hovering around the frame of the lantern. Others flutter down from inside it. The panes of the lantern are stained yellow so that even on dull days the light that filters through assumes the tone of sunlight.

This lively, sensuous form of decoration was peculiar to Bernini. The sculptor in him could never for long refrain from introducing the human form, a proclivity which exposed him to the jibes of his contemporaries that he clearly preferred bodies to souls. In the drum of his dome at Castel Gandolfo he made *putti* support medallions of bas-reliefs over each window and a garland which likewise ran, or was draped round the perimeter. These delightful decorative accessories are the creation of Bernini the scene designer. At the Assunta at Ariccia, Bernini's third church for Pope Alexander on the central plan—which unlike that of Sant'

Andrea is a circle—the theatrical trimmings are modified, and there is no gold and no marble. The coffers of the dome are of plain stucco. But then the Assunta is in every respect a less sumptuous and a more tranquil composition. In perhaps no other building did Bernini show himself so confirmed a classicist under the inescapable, pervasive influence of the Pantheon.

When all is said and done the fact remains that Bernini was fundamentally a classicist. There is nothing about his plans and elevations at which Vitruvius, could he have seen them, would be able to cavil. The same cannnot be said about the work of his great contemporary and rival Borromini, who constantly and flagrantly transgressed the classical rules, while remaining possibly the greater architect of the two. Vitruvius would have been horrified by Borromini's licence. He would have been merely startled by Bernini's eccentricities which gave to accustomed classical façades a plasticity never imagined hitherto. For Bernini dressed old accepted forms in new garments. Only at times did his sense of fantasy lead him to commit surface extravagancies of a daring but diverting kind, such as the range of perspective openings on the central top storey of the Palazzo Barberini, or the six Chigi mountains perilously balanced on the tight-rope of a swag over the Porta del Popolo. These are merely superficial operations. He always respected and left severely alone the underlying classical matrix. Herein possibly lies Bernini's weakness, for his quirks and conceits were not always integrated with his architecture, but applied to decoration. Hence his interiors were sometimes more sculptural than truly architectural.

Since the influence Bernini exercised upon succeeding generations was immense, he was perhaps indirectly but unwittingly responsible for many decorative follies, particularly in France in the eighteenth and nineteenth centuries. His *putti* heads upon the dome and reclining youths upon the lintels of the windows inside Sant' Andrea have a masculine quality reminiscent of Michelangelo. When we see these transmuted by Charles Garnier into the insipid masks and languishing plaster hermaphrodites which sprawl around the Opera House at Monte Carlo, then we may feel tempted to blame the great genius who first applied baroque sculpture to backgrounds to which at times it bore no seeming relation. If so, then we are not being fair. We may just as well impute responsibility to Picasso for the deformities of his imitators. We must never overlook the fact that the astonishingly versatile Bernini was above all a sculptor of the first rank, whose decoration taken out of its context is by itself always interesting and usually of the highest artistic merit.

BIBLIOGRAPHY

M. ARMELLINI. *Le Chiese di Roma*, 1891.

Enciclopedia Italiana. Article on Bernini.

A. MUÑOZ. *G. L. Bernini*, 1925.

MARCEL RAYMOND. *Le Bernin*, 1911.

L'Encyclopédie. Article on Bernini by Quatremère de Quincy.

T. H. FOKKER. *Roman Baroque Art*, pl. 156 & pls. 118–21, 1938.

ROBERTO PANE. *Bernini Architetto*, 1953.

G. B. DE ROSSI. *Insignum Romae Templorum Prospectus*, 1684.

BAROQUE II

San Carlo Alle Quattro Fontane

FRANCESCO BORROMINI was only one year younger than Bernini and died thirteen years before him. He laid the foundation of the little church of San Carlo alle Quattro Fontane in 1638, exactly twenty years before Bernini began to build Sant' Andrea. Nevertheless San Carlino, as the church is usually called in accordance with Italian love of diminutives and terms of endearment, exemplifies a stage of the baroque style so far advanced beyond that of Sant' Andrea that it seems to be suitable to refer to Borromini's work after instead of before that of his great contemporary. Besides Borromini rather anticipates the spirit of the eighteenth century than expresses that of his own, which must always remain dazzled by the refulgence of Bernini's tremendous personality.

Although San Carlino was begun before Sant' Andrea it was one of the first essays and certainly the first entire work of Borromini's architecture. By this date Bernini had already built a good deal and his enormous prestige was firmly established. Borromini on the contrary enjoyed no comparable fame and outside a small circle of artists his gifts were practically unrecognized. He was indubitably a slow developer. Besides he had none of the worldly ambitions and none of the push of Bernini. His temperament, in surprising contradistinction to his art, displayed no bravura and none of the other's dynamic impulses. Outwardly he appeared a hesitant and diffident man. Yet inwardly he was all on fire. His portrait, I think, proclaims that his was a tormented soul. The highly sensitive face is strained and unhappy. There is anguish in his inward-looking eye and dismay in his parted, questioning lips. Throughout his life he was gnawed by a melancholy which in the end consumed him. In an ultimate access of despair, brought about by speculating on the meaning of existence, which to him was his art, he burnt all his drawings and stabbed himself to death with a poniard. Simple, ascetic and devout, Borromini laboured only for the glorification of his God through the perfection of his art. He lived virtuously and studiously, a solitary hypochondriac under the ever darkening canopy of doubt and self-depreciation. How different then was his temperament to that of his extrovert, buoyant, self-confident and hedonistic rival.

I have already stressed that the important point to be remembered about Bernini's architecture is its basically correct classicism. Although so often his gift for virtuosity, his love of novelty and his hatred of simplicity led him to invest his buildings with strange sculptural forms, his architecture nevertheless remained unimpeachably Vitruvian underneath. Borromini's buildings by contrast were anything but correct according to renaissance standards. They broke all the Vitruvian rules which the scholars of the fifteenth century had piously codified and laid down as sacrosanct. Yet although his architecture was far more eccentric than Bernini's it seldom resorted to extraneous decorative motifs. The more outrageous it became, the less did it depend upon ornament for effect. The extravagance lay in the basic architecture itself. Hence Borromini was bolder and more original than Bernini. The game he played was naturally a more perilous one. In taking the liberties he did with those architectural principles which had been proved throughout centuries of experience both by the ancient and the modern worlds, he ran the risk of terrible pitfalls. The ethical school of Ruskinian critics honestly believed and vehemently proclaimed that he fell into them headlong. You too may believe the same thing. I do not. I believe Borromini to have been the most revolutionary Roman architect to work in the classical idiom, and also the most disarming: revolutionary because he was the first deliberately to break with Vitruvian rules by twisting and distorting the orders into shapes hitherto undreamt of: disarming because, try as you will, you may never catch him out in charlatanry. He always keeps within the bounds of reason, however close to the winds of insanity he sails. His compositions invariably retain that balance and rhythm essential to good architecture. Proportion, Borromini said, was the divine gift to man, having its origin in the body of Adam which was made by the hand of God. Consequently, he continued, painters and sculptors, familiar with the human body, made the best architects because they knew how to fashion buildings into true living forms. His regard for proportion never wavered. Later baroque architects and rococo decorators were to be just as poetical as Borromini. The buildings of Guarini and Juvara in and around Turin were more speculative; those of Fischer von Erlach in Vienna were more fanciful and insubstantial. The buildings of Valvassori in Rome and of the brothers Asam in Bavaria were more fantastic and unreal. Bold or timid, aetherial or ponderous, virtuous or immoral, judge them by whatever standard you choose, whether in Dresden, Prague, Madrid, Saint Petersburg, or in the cities of Spanish America, they all derive from Borromini who was the first so intrepid as to inaugurate a schism in the classical tradition, productive of the rarest beauties, but—such is the nature of schisms which are not destroyed root and branch —surely responsible for the ultimate disintegration of architecture in our own day.

Borromini was the son of an architect in the service of the house of Visconti. Born on the Lake of Lugano he spent his boyhood learning to be a sculptor in Milan. At the age of sixteen he fled to Rome where like Bernini he remained for the rest of his life. In the seventeenth century schools of sculpture and architecture did not exist and students habitually learnt their art in the workshops of established masters upon whom parents felt they had some claim of kinship. The young Borromini was fortunate in having a cousin, Carlo Maderna, who was chief architect to the

Vatican and the creator of the nave and façade of Saint Peter's. Accordingly he became apprenticed to this cousin just as the cousin in his youth had been apprenticed to an uncle, Domenico Fontana. Until he was thirty Borromini worked as a mere mason helping to cut and carve stone and marble for the basilica. He became deeply attached to Maderna at whose death he expressed the wish to be buried eventually in the same tomb. But sincere devotion to a master who was a product of the Counter-Reformation did not prevent the apprentice developing a passion for the works of Michelangelo. At the Vatican he had every facility for studying what became of course the chief inspirations of his own art.

After Bernini had in 1629 succeeded Maderna as papal architect, Borromini continued for four years to serve the Vatican in his old capacity. But the interlude was not a happy one. Bernini in a high-handed manner which was his second nature, treated the master mason as an underling, and Borromini was too modest a colleague to assert the independence of his position. The official architect considered the mason's designs to lack tradition and to be raw and mannered. At last in 1633 the opportunity arose for the mason to shake off the tutelage of his arrogant task master. Borromini was offered the post of architect to the University of the Sapienza. After certain misgivings he accepted it. Even so his duties to the University were of a routine kind and many years elapsed before he was called upon to design for the authorities the chapel of Sant' Ivo.

Beyond an occasional window and doorway at the Vatican and at Pope Urban's great family palace of the Barberini, Borromini had built nothing before his fortieth year. His art which was to become so revolutionary in its effects took a long time to mature. His cautious disposition as well as his circumstances prevented the modest mason from rejecting sooner the academic style which his revered master Maderna had only seldom and then very gently flouted. Besides it was not easy for a man of a diffident and hesitant nature to find patronage and scope to build in the disturbing style which he was now evolving. How it came about that the secluded order of Trinitarians, devoted to the redemption of Christian slaves in the custody of infidel Moors, gave him his first commission is not explained. But they did so, and he built for them first a refectory (now the sacristy), then the cloisters, then the nave, and lastly, thirty years later, the façade of the church of San Carlino.

The façade of San Carlino is what we are going to see first. But to look at it properly is an awkward procedure. The best time of the week to choose is early on a Sunday morning when the hectic traffic at the cross roads where the church is sited has not reached the hideous density which is maintained throughout every hour of every other day. The best approach is down the Via del Quirinale from Sant' Andrea, a few hundred yards away to the south-west. This is the only route to allow a glimpse of the cupola with its concave faces, stepped lantern and ball precariously perched on the summit. Borromini was particularly fond of this composition which he reproduced at Sant' Andrea delle Fratte, where it is too skied to be seen comfortably, and to greater advantage upon the dome of Sant' Ivo. It was widely and variously copied upon German churches in the succeeding century and illustrated as an almost indispensable crowning feature by Paulus Decker the elder in his extraordinary plates of architectural fantasies.[1] It was even followed in a modified form by Thomas Archer upon the tower of Saint Philip's, Birmingham. It was of course an adaptation of the Temple of Venus at Baalbec where detached columns round the body carry a cornice made to sweep back in segmental curves. At Baalbec the purpose of the design was functional, to meet the difficult junction of the entablature of a circular body with that of a rectangular portico. By Borromini it was simply used to satisfy his need for curves.

The site of San Carlino is very splendid on the ridge of the

[1] Published in Augsburg, 1711–16.

Quirinal Hill. It comprises the south corner formed by the crossing of two straight streets with distant vistas, terminating in the obelisks of La Trinità de' Monti and the Quirinal, the Porta Pia and the campanile of Santa Maria Maggiore. Each of the four corners of the cross roads is canted so as to shelter under an arch a delightful rococo fountain. Nevertheless the twentieth century has done its utmost to spoil the site. The building over the fountain of the north angle has been torn down and a spider's web of trolley-bus wires has been contrived at the crossing to make every view of the church as difficult as possible during those rare seconds when the flow of traffic does not screen it.[2] There are but two stances from which to look at the church in safety. One is the iron rail which protects the north fountain of Fidelity, reclining on her right elbow. You may perch upon the rail close to the marble hound which adores its mistress with languishing eyes and confronts old Tiber lying under an ilex and holding a cornucopia. From this coign of vantage you can take in the main and side elevations and admire the clever way in which the architect has capped the angle face with a concave turret and steeple. The disadvantage of this position is that the morning sun has a habit of streaming down the narrow Via delle Quattro Fontane straight into your eyes. The second stance is in the Via del Quirinale directly opposite the entrance of the church. There on the pavement you may flatten your back against a palace façade. The disadvantages of this position are twofold. It does not enable you to see the side elevation of the church and it is rather uncomfortable. The pavement at this point is not wide and the pedestrians are immensely curious why you are staring and somewhat indignant that you are getting in their way.

The front of San Carlino has, like much baroque architecture of an advanced sort, aroused extreme censure and

---

[2] Today the measure of a man's aesthetic sense is the extent to which he notices and minds overhead wires (trolley bus, telephone, electricity, television, etc.). If he is able to ignore them he is a happy philistine. If not, then he is indeed unfortunate, for all visual enjoyment of architecture and landscape has been vitiated for him within the last fifteen years, or so.

extreme eulogy. It seems as though this particular style must invite the most unbalanced judgments from eclectic and otherwise level-headed critics. In the seventeenth and eighteenth centuries the Baroque did not have this effect, and cultivated persons were able to view it dispassionately, although to their eyes it was a novel and one would suppose, a correspondingly outrageous style. Tobias Smollett's judgment, for example, was not profound but it was favourable. He called San Carlino "a singular fabric for neatness, of an oval design, built of a new white stone; the columns are worth notice." Doubtless this opinion which was expressed in 1763, was shared by the majority of English gentlemen in Rome in the middle of the eighteenth century when the Baroque had long been the generally accepted style. It almost looks as though Smollet thought the church had only just been erected, so little change in architectural taste had there been within the past hundred years. In the mid nineteenth century the sentiments of English visitors towards the Baroque were of course completely reversed. To them it was anathema and represented Jesuitry, the Inquisition, the Whore of Babylon and whatever moral depravity their ethical standards associated with bad architecture. The views of Charles Dickens on San Carlino, if he ever cared to express them, may be guessed from his pronouncement that the works of Bernini and Borromini "are, I verily believe, the most detestable class of productions in the wide world." Throughout the nineteenth century this violent antipathy towards the Baroque was maintained in conservative circles. In a book on baroque architecture by one of our more prominent architectural historians alive today—published it must in fairness be stated over forty years ago—we read that San Carlino "has hardly a single point in its favour internally or externally . . . the plan of this church . . . falls far short of Wren's dazzling success in Saint Stephen Walbrook, and the façade is simply grotesque."[3]

[3] Martin S. Briggs—*Baroque Architecture*, 1913.

With the lapse into architectural anarchy between the two world wars fashionable opinion of the Baroque (I purposely do not include the Rococo) veered to the opposite extreme. In the stormy disintegration of styles the Baroque was something sympathetic which could be apprehended. Here was a manner of building which apparently lacked all those qualities which the inter-war generation found distasteful—tradition, discipline, proportion—and combined those qualities which on the other hand it deemed cosmopolitan and modish—independence of rules, profligacy and prettiness. Accordingly the Baroque could safely be lauded to the skies, whereas the High Renaissance was despised as dull and the Gothic (with the tolerable exception of the Strawberry Hill variety) positively spurned.

How suspicious we should be of fashionable enthusiasm for one style which necessarily implies disparagement of every other: how inanely wrong were the reasons for which the last generation blandly admired the Baroque: how fatuous were the qualities which they read into the best baroque buildings. For in reality the virtues they pretended to see in it no more existed than the vices with which the Victorians had invested it half a century earlier.

There is of course nothing haphazard about the façade of San Carlino. On the contrary it proclaims the immense amount of thought which the architect put into it. Its every element, every detail has conscientiously been sifted and sorted out, before application. Its failure—and it is a failure, because as an entity it really cannot be called beautiful—is due to an over concentration of purpose. Drawings in the Albertina, Vienna, show that Borromini made numerous preliminary sketches before hitting upon the final design. The work was his last, actually finished just after his death, and who knows that it was not even the cause of that terrible despair which overwhelmed him at the end. He expended too much deliberation and lavished every resource at his command upon it, as though he knew his inspirations were about to be exhausted and his life was draining to the dregs. He did not succeed in integrating units which taken by themselves are intensely interesting and, surprisingly enough, nearly all beautiful.

The façade is of two orders, both Composite. The strangely unconventional treatment of the capitals, swathed in acanthus leaves and festooned with little crowns is probably what gave rise to Smollett's remark that "the columns are worth notice." Each order is divided into three bays and embraces two stages. Of the lower order the middle bay is convex and the end bays are concave. The undulating contour that they consequently make is emphasized by an immoderately thick entablature, itself causing a movement sensuous and rhythmic. Within the three bays a lesser order contains the entrance door and two flanking oval windows, and supports three niches. The oval windows are features of fantastic beauty. They are balanced vertically on Roman sacrificial altars adorned with rams' heads, volutes and swags. The surrounds are composed of palm branches gathered into a crown of tongues of flame—a device much favoured by Borromini and used by him over the windows of the Sapienza palace. Unfortunately the lateral niches are too big and heavy for the windows below them and the statues they carry are poor. The central statue of San Carlo Borromeo over the door is a sentimental rendering of a man whose holy expression does little to mitigate features of offensive ugliness. His niche is shielded by a pair of cherubim—the tips of whose upraised wings fold over each other so as to form a protective ogival canopy—variants of those cherubim with wings folded across their bodies on the campanile of Sant' Andrea delle Fratte. The cherubim, unlike the statues, are masterpieces of sculpture.

Of the upper order the three bays are all made concave. This was a bold move on the part of Borromini and meant to play a melody contrapuntal to the theme of the lower order. But as though fearful of striking too strong a discord he relented somewhat by introducing the large oval frame into the apex and the curious little tambour-shaped pavilion

Sant' Andrea Al
Quirinale

San Carlo Alle Quatre
Fontane

under it. Thus he gave to his central bay a degree of that convexity so emphatic in the corresponding bay of the lower order. The introduction of the oval frame—of which the picture and canvas are now quite perished—supported by two flying angels is a rare instance of Borromini resorting to elements extraneous to his architecture. It is the sort of thing Bernini frequently did to great effect in his interiors. Here it is a detraction from the architecture. The ogival crest with its inverted scrolls behind the frame is moreover unhappily related to the parapet beside it. The little pavilion on the other hand is very delightful. It has a door-window giving on to a balcony. It was doubtless suggested to Borromini by engravings of the pavilion on the upper stage of the rock tomb of the Khasne at Petra, which likewise occupies a central position between bays flanked by Corinthian columns.

Antonio Muñoz writing during the inter-war years praised this façade as "*un miracolo . . . e rivela già tutte le caratteristiche dell' arte borrominiana, la novità della concezione, la nota personale in ogni minuto particolare, la fantasia inesaurabile che accumula idee su idee, con facilità, con liberalità prodigiosa, senza sforzo, senza stento.*" He was the first critic of our time properly to rehabilitate the genius of Borromini, whom in the access of his enthusiasm—Borromini was his favourite of all artists—he exalted on occasions beyond desert. Muñoz was right in tracing here all the characteristics of Borromini's art and the quintessence of his spirit. In fully admitting the facility, the prodigality, the apparent effortlessness of the architect's invention, I must deplore it too. I cannot help finding his inexhaustible fantasies piled too thickly one upon another. The façade is too concentrated to be digestible. And as I said before, it fails to be wholly beautiful.

Notwithstanding my advice at what time of the week to study the outside of San Carlino, a Sunday morning, when continuous Masses are being said and sung, is, I need hardly point out, an unsuitable occasion to see the inside of the church and monastery. Since the objections to looking at the

Trevi Fountain

exterior on weekdays no longer apply, you may as well
choose any morning except a Sunday to go indoors. You will
very probably find the main door locked, for the reason that
San Carlino is not a parish church but the private chapel of
the Trinitarian Order to which in courtesy it admits the
public for worship. And after nine o'clock the last weekday
Mass will have been celebrated. This does not mean that
you cannot go inside. But it does necessitate asking permission.
You must ring the bell at the door to the right of the church.
This is the entry to the monastery. It was from here that in
November, 1848, the first attack was launched by Garibaldi's
revolutionaries, who had seized the monastery, against the
Quirinal Palace, causing the flight of Pius IX from Rome
and the downfall of his government. From a window over
the door the shot was fired which killed Monsignor Palma,
one of the Pope's secretaries and an eminent ecclesiastical
historian, seated at a window opposite. It is an incident of
which the Trinitarians do not much care to be reminded.
Soon after you have rung, one of the Brothers in sandals
and a white hooded habit, with a red and blue cross on the
breast, will come to the door. He will be very polite without
speaking, for the Order is a silent one, and with an assenting
wave of the hand will permit you to roam around at your
leisure.

You step straight into the minute cloisters. They are of
two colonnaded walks one above the other, enclosing a
court and central octagonal well-head. The plan of the
cloisters is rectangular with convex angles treated in an
ingenious manner, simple and picturesque. In the lower
walk Tuscan columns are made to carry wide semicircular
headed openings between narrow ones under flat lintels.
The upper walk repeats the arrangement of alternate wide
and narrow openings, but without any arches. The curious
octagonal bell-shaped capitals of the columns carry a
continuous architrave. The balustrade of the upper walk
repeats the convexity of the angles of the lower. The pear-
shaped balusters are cut into three faces and alternately

reversed so as to bulge now at the bottom, now at the top. The whole composition, like the surface of the sea after a storm, sustains a gently swelling movement without breaking into jagged irregularities.

From the cloisters you pass to the sacristy, which is another work of art and perhaps the first room Borromini ever designed. The carvèd aumbries for vestments, in cutting across the perspective apse somewhat spoil the proportions of the room which was originally meant for a refectory. The faintest shadows of pilaster heads cause hardly perceptible breaks in the entablature which traces the sinuous contour of the walls. In place of capitals plumes of acanthus and at the four corners angel heads with outspread wings (variants this time of those which Borromini set in flight upon the aisle roofs of Saint John Lateran) support the entablature and remarkable vaulted ceiling. Here the thick plaster ribs spring into groins and C scrolls linked by masks wearing feathered headdresses. The walls are washed a buttercup yellow and grass green, the frieze and ceiling sky blue and the plaster-work snow white, probably the traditional colour scheme of this extraordinary and surely most engaging gothico-rococo apartment.

You may walk into the church from the sacristy which is placed at its east end, but I do not recommend this approach. The Trinitarian Brothers will be rather bewildered when you beg them to let you out into the street and then to unlock the west door of the church so that you may come in again by this roundabout route. But it is worth while risking a little embarrassment in order to acquire your first impressions of the interior as the architect intended. These impressions are diametrically different to those you experienced on entering Sant' Andrea. There they were of colour, opulence and space; here they are of chiaroscuro, austerity and confine-ment. There the plan was revealed at once as oval and straightforward; here it seems at first muddled and un-controlled. Although the walls and columns are a uniform white, the church is dim, for the only reluctant light

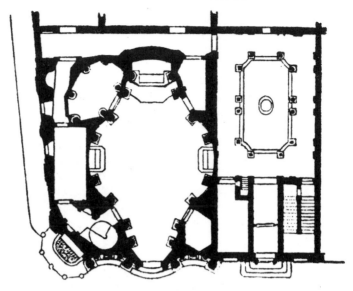

trickles through the small cupola and west window over the organ. The mystery and gothic gloom is not dispelled by the watery blue and grey ribs of the marble floor, the dull gold frames of the heavily varnished pictures by Maratta or the bronze wreaths over the doorheads. In other words there is nothing sumptuous or theatrical about the interior. The pictorial effects are not brought about by superfluous decoration but by a fugue of architectural parts, of which the harmonizing themes are vertical elevations and a truly masterly play of concavities.

The plan which does not make itself immediately apparent is admittedly a trifle involved, but it is rational. It is an ellipse with ends compressed so as to resemble the shape of a lemon. Yet the ends do not, as you might expect, produce interior convexities where they are compressed. Out of contrariness or daredevilry I fancy, Borromini meant to avoid this natural sequence, and fashioned concavities instead. He rejoiced in a contradiction of geometrical rules, as of Vitruvian precedents. Certainly he was astonishingly original, and at times his conceptions are more ingenious than impressive, and have to be looked for. For instance, not every visitor to the church of Sant' Ivo will discover that Borromini made the plan in the shape of a bee, complete with folded wings, tail, feet, head and even antenae, in honour of the Barberini pope whose crest this insect was. The intention is only apparent to the initiated, and then on paper, for with unerring taste and skill the architect nevertheless contrived that the nave of Sant' Ivo was a regular hexagon of apses. Ingenuities such as these must be regarded as amusing conceits (in the mannerist tradition) like anagrams in poetry. From the hands of lesser artists they are not always so amusing, and the plan of Thomas Archer's pavilion at Wrest Park in Bedfordshire adds nothing to its beauty by following the contours of a housefly.

In devising the interior of San Carlino Borromini was not obliged to satisfy the whim of a single patron, either prince or pope. It is fairly certain that the Trinitarians did not interfere with his object, unconventional though it was, of creating an illusion of height and length and of density of columns by means of his lemon-like plan. Considering the extremely restricted site—the guide books assure you that the whole area covered by church, cloisters and monastery corresponds with that of one of the four piers supporting the dome of Saint Peter's—the architect's make-believe is almost miraculous. The beauty of the interior may fall short of Wren's incomparable Saint Stephen Walbrook, which is square in plan (aesthetic comparisons are always invidious and usually senseless), but Borromini's victory over a recalcitrant site is every whit as remarkable. For what he set out to achieve was a paradox, namely the impression of a basilican plan, where, on account of the limited area, only a central plan was permissible. It is one of Borromini's claims to greatness that in spite of the prevailing contempt of his age for the mediaeval he admired gothic verticality.

The entrance to Sant' Andrea is from one of the middle points of the circumference of the ellipse; to San Carlino it is from one of the sharp ends.[4] When you stand just inside the doorway you are positively obliged to take in the architect's intention or else entirely fail to grasp the meaning of this astonishing interior. The range of vision, restricted though it be, is as compulsive to your eye as a railway track to an engine. You simply must follow it obediently from one end to the other. The sixteen Composite columns ranged on either side the nave drag your eye to the focal point of the high altar opposite you. From where you stand the columns appear to be set at irregular intervals. The illusion is caused by the series of concavities within the ellipse. These are emphasized by the continuous entablature with its unadorned frieze running over the columns like a clean line made by the pollarded tops of an avenue of plane trees. And plane trees are what the creamy columns, in their seemingly irregular setting, recall to my mind. At your western apse they appear densely assembled, then they spread out gently on either side of you into the greatest diameter of the oval, to close again, their smooth boles pressed together before the eastern apse of the high altar. Here a trick of perspective adds to the unreality of the scene. Under a semicircular arch a half dome contains a range of coffers so disposed as to give a greater impression of depth than exists, the closer you approach it. By the same process the pediment over the entablature subsides from a tight ogee practically into a horizontal line like a flag being slowly unfurled.

The sense of movement is so convincing that it is almost disturbing. No single feature of the church seems to keep still for an instant. You have only to shift the weight of your body from one foot to the other for columns to alter their position and curves their contours. The pedestals under the columns and the abaci (shallow blocks) over the capitals are curved to follow the concavities of the church's plan. The capitals themselves are adorned with waving acanthus

[4] J. B. Fischer von Erlach at the Karlskirche, Vienna (1715–37) followed the San Carlino arrangement of entry at one of the sharp ends of an elliptical nave, under an elliptical dome.

leaves and eccentric reversed volutes of a sort imitated by Thomas Archer and the Bastard brothers in the west of England a hundred years later. In the perpetual twilight the roots of the plane trees seethe like serpents and the foliage of their branches wriggles like worms. Even the niches between the columns are alive, their shell heads either aflame with tongues of fire or quivering like the pleated skirts of jelly-fish. The oak confession boxes are by no means as quiet as their purpose demands, for the front of each is serpentine and the pediment curved like the lash of a whip. Moreover upon the forehead of each is painted in gold the all-seeing eye of God which follows your own with a relentless, reprehensive gaze.

The spandrels (i.e. the spaces in the ceiling between the arches) contain biblical scenes in stucco relief within frames. They are supported by the wings of Borromini's favourite cherubim joined tip to tip to form an ogee, but what the shape of the frames may be it is impossible to determine, for wherever you move they change from circles into ovals, and then into pears. Their delusive shapes are governed by the semicircular and elliptical arches of the apses and the oval of the cupola which confine the frames. The cupola covers the greater part of the nave. It is pitted with recessed coffers in a variety of pentagonal shapes, and the cross of the Trinitarians. The great depth and crisp moulding of the coffers induce sharp contrasts of light and shadow. The cornice on to which the cupola neatly fits like the lid of a tin sprouts a serried row of acanthus and honeysuckle crests whose vegetable quality is more naturalistic than refined. The oval lantern crowning the cupola is encircled with an inscription in clear letters to the honour of the Most Holy Trinity and Blessed Charles Borromeo, and the date 1640. The underneath of the lantern displays within a frame of convexities the Holy Ghost in a blaze of concentrated light, which, however, is so diffused in its descent that even on the brightest days the mystical dimness of the interior is not dispelled.

And now in unexpected disregard of symmetry are two

irregular chapels, attached like growths to the carefully proportioned body of San Carlino. Their presence, however, causes no disturbance to the visible plan, for they are carved out of those waste areas between the lemon of the nave and the street elevations, the one being entered by an opening on the right of the main entrance the other by a doorway to the left of the sanctuary. Their style is very different to that of the nave. It is surprisingly feminine, more rococo than baroque, more eighteenth century than seventeenth. The chapel next the sanctuary which is the larger and more ornate is shaped like a hexagonal chrysalis. Six fluted Corinthian columns are set upon concave bases at the six corners. The entablature rises into pediments, of which the lesser are pointed and the larger segmental, the under surfaces of the pediments being carved with palm leaves, as are the ribs of the vaulted and coved ceiling. The sculpture throughout is very sensitive. The chapel is more like an exotic boudoir than the shrine of an ascetic religious order. Robert Adam's little closets at the ends of the Long Gallery at Syon House designed for the Duchess of Northumberland's dalliance were not more elegant and exclusive. If ever you wished to trace rococo decoration of the eighteenth century back to an ultimate source I believe the scholars would be hard driven to dispute it in these two chapels of Borromini.

Mr. Fiske Kimball who is the most recent scholar to write at length about the rococo style would not presumably entertain this suggestion for a moment.[5] In his immensely recondite book he sets out to prove that the origin of the Rococo is not Italian, but French, and can be attributed to certain chimneypieces designed by Pierre Lepautre at the palace of Marly for Louis XIV between 25th April and 10th June, 1699. He is nothing if not precise. He argues that the style of these chimneypieces and of subsequent designs of Lepautre[6] have no precedents either in France or for that

[5] Fiske Kimball—*The Creation of the Rococo*, 1943.
[6] For apartments at Versailles and the Trianon, the choir stalls at Orléans Cathedral, the altars and furnishings of the chapel at Versailles, and the choir stalls and altar of Nôtre Dame.

matter in Italy. Lepautre, he tells us, never went to Italy and in any case after Bernini's abortive visit to Paris in 1665 the Italian Baroque was held at a grave discount in France. For over thirty years a classical reaction fostered by Colbert as *Surintendant des Bâtiments du Roi*, produced building and decoration in a severe academic style. Mr. Fiske Kimball, who is well aware that for a quarter of a century before Bernini's Paris visit the Italian baroque style had reigned in France, implicitly denies it the paternity of Lepautre's Rococo.

This would be all very fine if Mr. Fiske Kimball had been able to convince us in what fundamental respects the style of the Marly chimneypieces differed from the Baroque. It is true that he speaks repeatedly of the French Rococo embodying "absolute artistic values of a new order," of it having replaced the "spatial and plastic energy" of the Baroque by something wholly different, i.e. "a flowing organization of line and surface," and he stresses its ultimately astylar character. The Rococo, he points out, gradually discarded the use of column and pilaster and reduced the projection of various moulds. But these definitions are not sufficiently primary to determine causal differences between two architectural styles. Besides, a mere glance at, say, Lepautre's design for the altar at Nôtre Dame shows that it must certainly have been inspired by Bernini's baroque baldaquins at Saint Peter's and the Val de Grâce. Again, his design of the Grand Salon at Marly does not differ in more than detail from that of Bernini's projected interior of Santa Maria di Montesanto. In both compositions the basic scheme of a main order under an attic, the tall openings flanking a doorway on the pediment of which figures recline, and the heavy swags and *putti* over the upper windows, are very similar in pattern and motif. It is impossible to believe that Lepautre and his followers of the early eighteenth century, Oppenord, Vassé, Meissonier and de Cotte were not considerably influenced by current engravings of the buildings of baroque architects in Italy, or that Colbert's academic interval in France meant more than a pause in the inevitable transition from French Baroque to French Rococo. We know, for instance, that in England the much longer interval, brought about by Wren's working life, between the Palladianism of Inigo Jones and its revival by Lord Burlington, did not break the continuity of that strictly classical evolution.

The truth is that the French raised the Rococo to heights of refinement which it never attained in Italy. It was an artistic manifestation in which they excelled all other European nations. In the eighteenth century French Rococo assumed a national quality distinct from that of the Italian peninisula. It was more feminine and fanciful. It reflected the life style of the court of Versailles, not the celibate functions of the Quirinal and Vatican palaces. But that it derived from seventeenth-century Italy and in particular from the two chief exponents of the Roman Baroque, namely Bernini and Borromini, we shall continue to maintain until more specific disproof is forthcoming than what Mr. Fiske Kimball has provided up to date.

BIBLIOGRAPHY

A. Muñoz. *Roma Barocca*, 1919.
Enciclopedia Italiana. Article on Borromini.
Maria Venturi Perotti. *Borromini.*
A. Muñoz. *Borromini*, 1920.
M. Armellini. *Le Chiese di Roma*, 1891.
Hans Sedlmayr. *Die Architektur Borrominis*, 1930.
G. C. Argan. *Borromini*, 1952.
S. Giedion. *Space, Time and Architecture*, 1954.

ROCOCO

———◦◎◦———

Trevi Fountain

WHAT exactly is the meaning of Rococo? If for a moment we overlook Mr. Fiske Kimball's panegyrics we find that the established authorities are unsparing in their condemnation of it. "Old fashioned, antiquated," the *Oxford Dictionary* calls it, "having the characteristics of . . . conventional shell- and scroll-work and meaningless decoration; tastelessly florid or ornate." These are positive, if provocative definitions. But the *Encyclopedia Britannica* is still more unfavourable. "Literally 'rock-work,' " it begins indignantly, as if to be termed rock-work is generally accounted the severest reproof to which any object with artistic pretensions can lay itself open. "A debased style at the best, essentially fantastic and bizarre," it continues. What then, one wonders, can it possibly be termed at the worst? And why is it necessarily debased to be fantastic and bizarre? "It ended in extravagance and decadence," says the *Encyclopedia Britannica*. But when and how one asks in bewilderment? And then one recalls how it did end—in the Vierzehnheiligen in Franconia, the Trinity Column in the Graben, Vienna, and in the staircase of the Bishop's Palace at Bruchsal. The airy, fairy German churches, pillars and palaces of the mid-eighteenth century may perhaps have been extravagant, but decadent? The word is inept, for these buildings are undeniably beautiful, and beauty and decadence are incompatible quantities.

"A meaningless mixture of imitation rock-work," the *Encyclopedia* now thunders, and always this terrible indictment of rock-work—"shells, scrolls and foliage, the word came eventually to be applied to anything extravagant, flamboyant, or tasteless in art, or literature." Now I persist in finding shells, scrolls and foliage in themselves charming and pretty. "The very exuberance of the rococo forms is, indeed, the negation of art. . . . Everything, indeed, in the rococo manner is involved and tortured. . . ." On and on it goes, until one can bear it no longer and must turn to some other authority.

So in the desperate hope of learning what the Rococo really is one opens that authoritative work, *The Architecture of the Italian Renaissance* by Anderson and Stratton, scholars of repute and Fellows of learned institutions. After referring to the play of line which characterizes the baroque style, its clever welding together of varied plan forms and its independence of elaborate detail, architectural connotations which one can grasp and appreciate, the authors go on to say, "By such a standard can the Baroque be measured and furthermore be distinguished from the *pernicious* Rococo [the italics are mine], which invariably overstepped the bounds of good taste, so that it produced nothing of permanent value—unless it be claimed that its use in garden architecture is legitimate." By this grudging concession I take it that garden architecture (involving rock-work) cannot be serious architecture and that consequently the rococo style may be deemed suitable for gardens, since it presumably is not serious either. This then is the established view of the Rococo. It is rock-work. It is not serious. It is gay. It is therefore pernicious and not to be tolerated.

We all know today that these indictments are exaggerated. We may even suspect that they are insincere. It cannot be that the last generation which so deeply venerated the Baroque, really regarded the Rococo which—whatever it was—followed hard upon the heels of the other, with the distaste professed by the authorities just quoted. But if it did not, why, we may well ask, did it suffer such definitions clearly formulated as long ago as Ruskin's day if not before, to remain unmoderated? This is a question difficult to answer. All I can do is to examine that monument in Rome which must unquestionably be an example of the rococo style because it is fantastic and bizarre, and is composed of shells, scrolls, foliage, rock-work, and other "decadent" things besides. Then I must try to understand what there is in it that so particularly offended the aesthetic (or was it the ethical?) sensibilities of the nineteenth and early twentieth centuries, and make up my mind whether their condemnation of the Rococo was entirely prejudiced and silly, or whether it had some substance.

The fountains of Rome cannot of course be associated with one period of history rather than another. They are, as Goethe recognized, the immortal tongues through which the spirit of the eternal city has disclosed its secret when invoked. Since Rome first became a city they have in one shape or another given voice to a ceaseless chatter. The reign of Constantine claimed as many as one thousand three hundred and fifty-two fountains in the fourteen municipal regions, whose pure waters were brought across the Campagna by nineteen different aqueducts. Towards the end of the middle ages the aqueducts were ruinous and only a few fountains fed by springs were left flowing. The Renaissance, however, as you would expect of an age which turned from a savage towards a gentle mode of living, set about repairing the aqueducts and refashioning the disused fountain heads in a new architectural style. The Counter Reformation popes were the first to lavish money on fountain building. Gregory XIII who was determined to complete the layout of the piazza della Rotonda erected the elegant basin now in front of the Pantheon. The terrible Sixtus V who is said to have grown mild whenever he paused to gaze upon flowing water, erected the cumbersome Moses fountain in the piazza San Bernardo and Paul V the still more ambitious Fontana Paolina on the Janiculum, with its five triumphal arches and vast superstructure. From now on popes vied with their predecessors in embellishing fountains, which they considered the indispensable attributes of civilized existence. Clement X who was unable to sleep away from the sound of a fountain, commissioned Bernini to contrive one with a great deal of splashing in the closet next to his bedroom. The last public performance of Pius IX, just before the temporal rule of the papacy ceased for ever in 1870, was to release in the piazza di Termini the powerful jet from the Aqua Marcia, which this pontiff had reharnessed at vast expense for the benefit of his subjects of a bare ten days future allegiance.

The centuries which rejoiced most in fountains were the seventeenth and eighteenth. Furthermore the Rococo seemed more suited to fountain building than any previous style. The *Encyclopedia Britannica* would doubtless agree, but for reasons which I refuse to share. Fountains it would argue are frivolous things, so is the rococo style; therefore they are well matched, and good riddance to both. But I maintain, like Pope Sixtus V, that fountains gladden the heavy hearts of men and are therefore to be encouraged. The Rococo being as it were a reflection of the classical style in a pool of moving water, where straight lines are mirrored into a thousand refractions and sinuosities, is eminently the style through which to convey these particular delights. For the most part the fountains which the seventeenth and eighteenth centuries erected were not on the scale, as they were not of the sedateness of the Counter Reformation designs. They were less monumental, and as befitted the subject more intimate and lively. A single triton blowing through a conch, a stranded boat in the middle of a street, an upturned wine barrel or a pile of books were considered more appealing mediums than a portentous arch of triumph. As the Baroque merged into the Rococo so the fountains of Rome became more fanciful. Solitary basins, vases and urns were made to fling water in jets, volutes, fans and girandoles in which the southern sun reflected all the colours of the rainbow. By the middle of the eighteenth century a fountain arose which in ambition and scale transcended anything conceived hitherto. Yet it combined monumentalism with liveliness, and formality with fantasy. It expressed all the whimsicality of its age. It was in fact a palace dissolving into a fountain.

ROCOCO

Joseph Forsyth, whose *Remarks on Antiquities, Arts and Letters, during an Excursion in Italy in the Years* 1802 *and* 1803 Murray's Handbook to Rome loves to quote as if they were the Gospel and not the random ejaculations of a schoolmaster, "respectable and virtuous,"[1] but shockingly ignorant, described the Trevi fountain as "another pompous confusion of fable and fact, gods and ediles, aqueducts and sea-monsters." Now if there is one adjective the Trevi certainly does not deserve it is *pompous*, call it whatever else you like. "But the rock-work," Forsyth concedes somewhat to our surprise—he was less of a spoil-sport than the *Encyclopedia Britannica*—"is grand, proportioned to the stream of water and a fit basement for such architecture as a castel d'acqua required, not" and here he purses his lips again, "for the frittered Corinthian which we find there." The truth is that the Trevi fountain probably gives most of us, if we dare to be honest, more pleasure than all the preceding monuments which I have described. I suspect that it did to Forsyth, to Garner and Stratton, and, if they ever went to Rome, the compilers of the disingenuous entries in the *Oxford Dictionary* and *Encyclopedia Britannica*. These people would, however, sooner have died than admit it, for the reason that architecture to them was a solemn business and its purpose to elevate the mind, not to titillate the senses. Therefore a building which flagrantly, wilfully set out to give pleasure and nothing else, was immoral. And so they gave vent to pious strictures about the perniciousness of the Rococo.

The water which feeds the Trevi fountain has its source at Salone, eight miles east of Rome in the direction of Tivoli, and is called the Aqua Virgo after a young woman who first disclosed it to a band of Roman soldiers dying of thirst. Its name may also be significant of the fact that it is by far the purest of all the Roman waters. In 19 B.C. Marcus Agrippa, who had already laid on the Aqua Giulia to his public baths behind the Pantheon, brought it to Rome by means of aqueducts. The Aqua Virgo continued to function

[1] To quote the words of the introductory Life of the Author.

until Vitigern, King of the Visigoths cut the channel and stopped the supply in the sixth century. Not until the fifteenth century were the popes able to repair the immense additional damage to the aqueduct which had accrued during the intervening nine hundred years. Finally Alberti was commissioned to erect a great basin in the place of the long vanished Roman fountainhead. In the golden days of the Renaissance the Aqua Virgo was Rome's only source of pure water, apart from remnants of the Aqua Traiana, which supplied the fountains in Saint Peter's piazza and that of Santa Maria in Trastevere. Even so its flow into Alberti's basin was intermittent. For constant drinking purposes the city relied upon a few polluted wells and the Tiber waters, which in superstitious rivalry with those of Jordan, were venerated as beneficial to the health as well as spirit. In consequence epidemics were rife and periodically fatal to the citizens.

Under Urban VIII the project to replace Alberti's basin with a monumental fountain was inaugurated. It resulted over a century and a quarter later in the Trevi structure which we know. Urban instructed Bernini to prepare far-reaching plans to clear a suitable space by wholesale demolition of surrounding dwellings. The expense of the work was to be met out of a special wine tax. The news that the Pope was about to reduce the flow of wine in order to provide additional water was received by his subjects with much discontent. When it was learnt that the architect had obtained a licence to demolish the Tomb of Cecilia Metalla on the Appian Way and use the materials for the new fountain, discontent turned to such sharp protest that the vandalistic project had to be dropped. Meanwhile Bernini's plans and drawings of the proposed construction, already in an advanced stage, were shelved.

For a hundred years nothing further was done. Then in 1730 Lorenzo Corsini, an octogenarian of much determination, ascended the throne of Peter as Clement XII. To him is due the initial undertaking of the ultimate scheme which came into being. Nevertheless he did not live to see it completed. It was fraught throughout with vexations and frustrations. The smiling, cheerful fountain, the most light-hearted piece of architecture in Rome, was the outcome of thirty years travail and tears. After the second anniversary of his election Clement held a contest for a new design for the mouth of the Trevi waters. A number of the most distinguished artists competed and a design by Luigi Vanvitelli was chosen. The victorious competitor was told to proceed instantly with working plans. A month later, however, the Pontiff suddenly and unaccountably regretted his choice, cancelled the arrangements made with Vanvitelli and announced that after all the work was to be given to another. The new choice was a young Roman, called Niccolò Salvi, of whom little enough is known now but still less was known then, beyond a single achievement. This was an ingenious construction for a firework display in the piazza di Spagna, which the young man had devised a few summers previously and by which Pope Clement suddenly recollected that he had been captivated. The only other recorded work of Salvi is the alterations to the Palazzo Odeschalchi carried out many years after the Trevi fountain was begun. Oddly enough Salvi's partner on this occasion was Vanvitelli who presumably had forgiven the slight received over the incident of the Trevi competition. The Palazzo Odeschalchi was until Salvi and Vanvitelli altered it the masterpiece of Bernini's domestic architecture. Thus Salvi's two surviving works are connected with Bernini and, as I am about to emphasize, his small reputation was to some extent acquired at the expense of the other's genius.

Salvi's designs for the Trevi now repose among the archives of the Accademia di San Luca. There is no question that he was largely influenced by Bernini's sketch for a colossal fountain of which the central figure was Neptune drawn by sea horses. Bernini's project was as well known to him as for the previous hundred years it had been to his several predecessors who toyed with ideas of reproducing it. But Salvi was also influenced by Vanvitelli's design with which all of Rome was then very familiar, namely a palace of two storeys with a central frontispiece of Corinthian columns and two curved lateral stairways embracing a large basin and an allegorical figure of Rome. Salvi's resulting scheme was, then, a combination of Bernini's and Vanvitelli's designs, modified to suit the changed circumstances, and overlaid with motifs in the prevailing theatrical style—the Rococo—of which he was undoubtedly a successful exponent.

For thirty years the work dragged on, arrested at intervals by obstacles which to patrons and artists alike seemed insuperable. Funds ran out, and when more were collected the architect had interested himself in other work. Then Clement XII died. His successor, Benedict XIV, was no less determined to bring the work to a happy conclusion, and was to be no less disappointed. As the building proceeded so did Salvi's ambitions soar. He wished to make the piazza in front of the fountain grander than it was. He quarrelled with the sculptors involved, and acrimonious law suits were the result. His critics—for his commission had brought him enemies—made him unduly sensitive and self-important. Benedict's patience became more and more strained. It received a terrible and unexpected relaxation in the sudden death of the architect in 1751. His own death followed seven years later. Still the fountain was not finished. Carlo Rezzonico became Pope Clement XIII. By now it was really a case of putting the finishing touches to Salvi's details, all of which were clearly worked out on paper. With a final effort the fountain was ready in 1762, to be acclaimed by the Romans a glory to their city. Clement XIII enjoyed the credit for a monument which had cost his predecessors so much sweat and expense. The story of the Trevi's agonized gestation may be read in the three succinct inscriptions recording the parts played by the pontiffs whose reigns had spanned it.

The whole south façade of the Palazzo di Poli has been given over to Salvi's composition. The façade taken by itself is not distinguished, and it is curious that James Gibbs who saw it before the rock-work and statuary were applied, should have praised it as a magnificent piece of modern architecture. Indeed judged as an artistic composition, and not as a theatrical backcloth it is frankly poor. It shows how a stage-decorator or contriver of firework-displays does not necessarily make an accomplished architect. Salvi has attempted to follow the theme of Michelangelo's twin palaces of the Capitol, with the addition of a basement. The piano nobile and second floor are comprised within a giant Corinthian order of pilasters, supporting an entablature and attic floor. But Salvi has made three mistakes, of which Bernini and Borromini and even his well known German contemporaries, like Fischer von Erlach and Neumann would not have been guilty. He has made his attic far too shallow and omitted a crowning balustrade. He has carried the heads of his second floor windows beyond the level of the capitals into the main entablature. He has introduced a lesser entablature—which is perfectly legitimate—between the two storeys, but unlike Michelangelo on the Capitoline, forgotten to support it, and treated it as a kind of running course. Here then he has committed outstanding blunders, which are not redeemed by any compensating quality or charm. A slight rearrangement of units in an orthodox manner would not have lessened the fantasy of the rococo composition he was about to impose upon the façade, and would have avoided an effect of jostled and cramped features, imperfectly integrated.

In the middle of this extremely muddled face Salvi stuck the great frontispiece which by comparison is more satisfactory, because architecturally correct. But it is entirely unoriginal. It is of course the familiar Roman triumphal arch motif literally reproduced. It is actually the Arch of Titus (with a large niche in place of the opening) to which the entablature of the Arch of Constantine has been added.

In bringing the frontispiece forward Salvi has nevertheless related it to the incorrect palace façade by continuing the main Corinthian order and repeating the intercolumnar spaces in the side bays. He has introduced Ionic columns to carry the lesser entablature within the niche, but nowhere else.

All the rest is sheer delight, for in dressing up his scenery and presenting it in a progressive perspective of sculptural elements Salvi was a master. Here he has introduced to Roman architecture a novel decorative element indeed, a stage setting made not of ephemeral cardboard but of hard, enduring travertine. From the niche—and you will notice that in contrast with the highly decorated half-dome the background is severely plain to simulate open space—the colossal figure of Neptune is emerging. The dramatic movement is highly convincing in spite of the fact, which is best overlooked, that the equipage could not have passed through the narrow intercolumnar space. The god in swirling cloak like a sail filled with wind has one leg advanced and one arm stretched out. He is drawn on a colossal cockle-shell by two winged sea horses, led by tritons. The horses plunge in the water, which is made to fan from between their prancing feet as they throw back their heads and thrash the air with their forked tails. One of the tritons grapples with the bit of his beast, the other heralds his master's approach by blowing through a conch. The central group of figures was designed by G. M. Maini and worked by the sculptor Pietro Bracci, one of the competitors in Clement XII's original contest. In alcoves to the left and right of Neptune are statues of Abundance and Salubrity by Filippo Valle and above them panels in relief of Agrippa approving the design of the aqueduct and the Virgo pointing out the source of the waters to the Roman soldiers, both by Andrea Bergondi. Over each of the four Corinthian columns stands a mythological figure, and, dominating the attic, winged genii support the arms and papal tiara of the Corsini, Clement XII. None of the sculptors employed, with the exception of Maini, was more than mediocre and their names are only remembered for the vexations and delays they caused the architect. Apart from a certain swagger in the pose of Neptune all the figures are stiff and devoid of inspiration. They help to adorn the scenery and proclaim their allegory, but are no more works of art than are those mascots, emblematic of speed upon the bonnets of motor-cars.

The rusticated basement floor of the palace merges with the imitation rock-work upon which it is meant to be founded. Salvi adopted this conceit from the angle bases of the palace which Bernini began (and never finished) for Constanza Pamphili, the neice of Innocent X, on Monte Citorio. So the left corner pilaster has been set on a projecting rock from the crevices of which in spring-time natural vetch and yellow compositae mingle with the travertine shrubs and weeds of Salvi's invention. The counterfeit plants are carved growing from the rock and shrouding with their thick foliage the leftmost basement window and corner pedestal. A small tree is fashioned under the right-hand column of the frontispiece and a water-worm in the act of gliding from under a leaf. By the side of the road an uncarved and worn block of entablature has been discarded with consummate negligence. Elsewhere a cartouche bearing a lion rampant has fallen carelessly upon a piece of rock. Beside it lies a cardinal's hat with tassels loosely suspended. On the extreme right of the composition stands a large urn half carved out of a jutting rock for no apparent reason. Actually it was set there on purpose to screen a group of envious artists who habitually gathered at a small café in order to criticize and jeer at Salvi whenever he was directing his workmen from this spot. For nothing is more vastly irritating to onlookers than the spectacle of a man, who in disregarding all the rules of his profession, nevertheless achieves a success.

And all the while water cascades before Neptune's cockle-shell into a chain of pools and spouts into the air from springs to dash in
　　　　　　　　　　　silver streams
Among the figured rocks, in murm'ring falls
Musical ever.

Finally the pools and rivulets are gathered into the great marble basin where the tourists throw their coins and little stippled waves, such as one seldom sees in nature but which Botticelli painted in the *Birth of Venus*, reflect upon the undersides of the grottoes. The restless hiss of the galloping water is accompanied by the clamour of voices from the men who stride the walls and railings at all hours of the day and night, summer and winter.

My conclusion is that the Trevi fountain is not good architecture. On the contrary it is poor. Salvi had not the vestige of an idea of the Vitruvian rules. But his deficiency in this respect gives you no ground for condemning the Trevi fountain as a composition base and disagreeable. It is of course nothing of the kind. It is admirable, not as architecture, but as stage setting, and it is extremely pretty, and extremely popular. You should not judge it by the standards which you assume in assessing the merits of the Tempietto. After all you did not judge those delightful Coronation arches in the Mall by the standards set by Kent's Horse Guards over the way. The Coronation arches were fanciful and gay: pictorial and miraculous. They made you gasp with alarm and wonder that they, so flimsy and unreal, stayed up as long as they did, resting their metal weight on points, like ballerinas poised on the tips of their toes. But they were not architecture. Architecture does not inspire such emotions. It should not cause you embarrassment; so that after a time you have to look away, because the law of gravity tells you it must soon, like the ballerinas if not allowed to rest, let out its breath and collapse in an ignominious heap. Ephemeral engineering may do that. So may the Eiffel Tower, pylons and houses made out of playing cards. Architecture should appeal as much to the intellect as poetry, and must seem to be enduring and eternal. The gothic, the renaissance, the baroque styles may evince this impression. The Rococo does not, simply because it is not an architectural style at all.

There is no use pretending that Roman Rococo was the

best Rococo in Europe. It never burst into that symphony of hilarity which characterized the movement in France during the last years of Louis XIV's reign and most of those of his great-grandson's, Louis XV, or in Southern Germany and Austria under the Emperor Charles VI. Indeed there is little in Rome—if we except the Trevi fountain and the Scala della Trinità, which incidentally was built at the expense of French patrons—to be called Rococo that is not rather an extension of the Baroque. Eighteenth-century palaces, like those of the Consultà, Corsini and Toni are more Baroque than Rococo. The fact is that by the eighteenth century Rome had for the second time in two thousand years (the first was during the middle ages) ceased to take the lead in architectural style. She has never yet resumed it. What she was henceforth to build in the neo-classical revival did not equal work in France, and even England, in that manner.

These reasons perhaps explain why Forsyth and successive critics down to our own generation instinctively mistrusted the Rococo. It was not an architectural style at all. But then they should never have treated it and judged it as one. That fault has been responsible for much harm to the cause of architecture. It may even have killed architecture stone dead. If we live long enough we may see its resurrection. At present there are few signs. Its death, or if you are optimistic, the trance in which it is now lapped was brought about largely by the Forsyth school expending so much hate on the Rococo that men were driven to revive by artificial respiration a series of outworn styles in desperate succession, Norman, Early Pointed, Moorish, Roman Baroque, Queen Anne, Louis Seize, Scottish Baronial and so forth. Not one of these short-lived styles was a true expression of its time and not one flourished naturally. And then in impatience and with contempt came the modernists, who not without reason exclaimed that architecture was moribund and must be swept away altogether. So it has been, and engineering with its hard, unyielding materials has taken its place.

To the old-fashioned stomach accustomed to architectural diet, steel and reinforced concrete and glass, which time can never season, are not digestible materials. But we must be sanguine. We have had proof that engineering can be made palatable when served in certain outrageous shapes and disguises. These may easily be discarded and quickly replaced, as the fleeting tastes of posterity dictate. Let us pray that they may become ever more ephemeral and—rococo.

BIBLIOGRAPHY

Luigi Càllari. *Le Fontane di Roma*, 1945.
C. Ricci. *Architettura Barocca in Italia*, 1912.
Fiske Kimball. *The Creation of the Rococo*, 1943.
W. J. Anderson & A. Stratton. *The Architecture of the Renaissance in Italy*, 1927.